POWER BI DAX

A Guide to Using Basic Functions in Data Analysis

Kiet Huynh

Table of Contents

CHAPTER I
Introduction to Power BI and DAX

1.1 Power BI - A Comprehensive Data Analysis and Visualization Tool

Welcome to the world of Power BI, a powerful and versatile data analysis and visualization tool developed by Microsoft. Power BI empowers organizations and individuals to connect to a wide range of data sources, transform raw data into meaningful insights, and create compelling visualizations that drive data-driven decision-making.

1.1.1 What is Power BI?

At its core, Power BI is a business analytics service that enables users to easily connect to various data sources, clean and transform data, and build interactive reports and dashboards. It provides a user-friendly and intuitive interface, allowing even non-technical users to harness the power of data analysis.

1.1.2 Data Visualization Capabilities

One of the key strengths of Power BI lies in its data visualization capabilities. With a vast array of charts, graphs, and interactive visualizations, users can bring their data to life and gain valuable insights at a glance. From simple bar charts to complex geographical maps, Power BI offers an extensive library of visuals to cater to diverse data analysis needs.

1.1.3 Seamless Data Connectivity

Power BI seamlessly integrates with various data sources, whether they are cloud-based or on-premises. Users can easily connect to popular services like Microsoft Excel, SharePoint, SQL Server, and other cloud-based platforms such as Azure, Google Analytics, Salesforce, and more. This flexibility ensures that data is always up-to-date and readily available for analysis.

1.1.4 Real-time Collaboration and Sharing

Collaboration is a crucial aspect of data analysis in any organization. Power BI allows users to share their reports and dashboards securely with colleagues, stakeholders, and decision-makers. The ability to collaborate in real-time fosters a data-driven culture, enabling teams to make faster and more informed decisions.

1.1.5 Mobile Accessibility

In today's fast-paced world, having access to data insights on the go is essential. Power BI's mobile app allows users to access their reports and dashboards from any mobile device, ensuring that critical information is always at their fingertips.

In conclusion, Power BI is an indispensable tool for modern data analysis and visualization. It empowers individuals and organizations to harness the power of data, gain insights, and make data-driven decisions. In the chapters that follow, we will explore Power BI in greater detail, including its integration with Data Analysis Expressions (DAX), to unlock even more advanced analytical capabilities. Let's dive in and discover the true potential of Power BI and DAX together!

1.2 DAX (Data Analysis Expressions) - Concepts and Role in Power BI

In our journey to explore the wonders of Power BI, we cannot overlook the essential role of Data Analysis Expressions (DAX). DAX is a powerful formula language that brings a whole new dimension to data modeling and analysis within Power BI. In this section, we will delve into the fundamental concepts of DAX and its crucial role in enhancing the capabilities of Power BI.

1.2.1 What is DAX?

Data Analysis Expressions (DAX) is a formula language designed specifically for Power BI and other Microsoft tools, such as Excel Power Pivot. DAX allows users to create custom calculations, measures, and calculated tables to perform dynamic data analysis and derive meaningful insights. Whether you need to calculate complex financial metrics, perform time-based analysis, or create sophisticated statistical measures, DAX has got you covered.

1.2.2 The Power of Calculation Context

At the heart of DAX lies the concept of calculation context, which is fundamental to understanding how DAX expressions work. Calculation context refers to the specific row, column, or cell context in which a DAX expression is evaluated. This context is dynamic and changes based on user interactions, such as filtering, drilling down, or slicing data. Understanding calculation context is essential for creating accurate and context-aware calculations.

1.2.3 DAX Functions and Operators

DAX provides an extensive library of functions and operators to perform various data manipulations and calculations. From basic arithmetic functions like SUM, AVERAGE, and COUNT to more advanced statistical functions like VAR, STDEV, and RANKX, DAX empowers users to perform a wide range of analytical tasks. Additionally, DAX offers time intelligence functions like TOTALYTD, SAMEPERIODLASTYEAR, and DATEADD, enabling users to perform time-based analysis with ease.

1.2.4 Aggregation and Filtering with DAX

DAX allows users to perform aggregations on data by leveraging functions like CALCULATE, FILTER, and ALL. These functions enable users to filter and manipulate data dynamically, ensuring that calculated measures respond to the changing context accurately. With DAX, users can perform complex calculations that consider various filters and relationships in the data model.

1.2.5 Relationships and DAX

Power BI relies on data relationships to connect different tables in the data model. DAX utilizes these relationships to perform seamless cross-filtering and enable data exploration across related tables. Understanding how DAX works with relationships is crucial for creating meaningful calculations that leverage data from multiple tables.

1.2.6 Time Intelligence with DAX

Time intelligence is a critical aspect of data analysis, and DAX excels in this domain. DAX provides a rich set of time-based functions, such as TOTALYTD, TOTALMTD, and DATESYTD, which enable users to perform year-to-date, month-to-date, and other time-related calculations effortlessly. These time intelligence functions are invaluable for performing trend analysis, comparing periods, and creating rolling averages.

In conclusion, DAX plays a pivotal role in extending the analytical capabilities of Power BI. With its powerful formula language, users can perform complex calculations, leverage aggregation and filtering, and explore time-based data with ease. By understanding the fundamental concepts and functions of DAX, users can create sophisticated data models and derive meaningful insights that drive smarter decision-making. As we proceed with our exploration of Power BI and DAX, we will delve deeper into practical examples and real-world applications, enabling you to unlock the full potential of this dynamic duo in the world of data analysis. So, let's continue our journey and dive deeper into the world of DAX and its seamless integration with Power BI!

As we embark on this journey into the world of Power BI and DAX, it is essential to define the objectives and scope of this book. Our primary goal is to equip readers with comprehensive knowledge and practical skills to harness the power of Power BI and utilize the full potential of DAX for data analysis and visualization.

1.3.1 Empowering Data Analysis and Visualization Skills

At the core of this book's objectives is empowering readers with the necessary skills to conduct data analysis and visualization effectively. We aim to provide a step-by-step approach to guide both beginners and experienced users through the process of connecting to data sources, transforming data, creating data models, and designing insightful reports and dashboards using Power BI.

1.3.2 Understanding DAX Concepts and Functionality

DAX is a key component of Power BI that unlocks the ability to create sophisticated calculations and measures. Our objective is to demystify DAX concepts and showcase its functionality, enabling readers to confidently work with DAX expressions to perform complex calculations, aggregations, and time-based analysis.

1.3.3 Applying DAX in Real-World Scenarios

Beyond theoretical knowledge, this book aims to bridge the gap between theory and practice by providing real-world scenarios and practical examples. Readers will learn how to apply DAX to solve common data analysis challenges and make informed business decisions based on data insights.

1.3.4 Creating Interactive and Dynamic Reports

Power BI is renowned for its interactive and dynamic reporting capabilities. Our book seeks to demonstrate how to leverage DAX to create interactive visuals, slicers, and filters that respond to user interactions, enabling users to explore data and gain deeper insights effortlessly.

1.3.5 Performance Optimization and Best Practices

Efficiency is paramount when dealing with large datasets and complex calculations. Our book includes guidance on optimizing DAX expressions and implementing best practices to enhance the performance of Power BI reports and dashboards.

1.3.6 Integration with Power Query and Power Pivot

To provide a comprehensive understanding of Power BI, we will explore the integration of DAX with Power Query and Power Pivot. Readers will learn how to leverage Power Query for data transformation and Power Pivot for building data models, while seamlessly integrating DAX for advanced calculations.

1.3.7 Target Audience

This book is designed for a diverse audience with varying levels of expertise. Whether you are a data analyst, business intelligence professional, data scientist, or a decision-maker seeking data-driven insights, this book caters to your needs. It is equally beneficial for beginners starting their Power BI journey and experienced users looking to deepen their DAX knowledge.

1.3.8 Prerequisites

While no prior experience with Power BI or DAX is required, a basic understanding of data analysis concepts and familiarity with Microsoft Excel or other spreadsheet software is advantageous. This book aims to be accessible to all readers and provides a solid foundation for those new to Power BI and DAX.

In conclusion, the objectives and scope of this book are to empower readers with the knowledge and skills to become proficient in Power BI and DAX. Through practical examples, real-world scenarios, and performance optimization tips, readers will be equipped to create dynamic and insightful reports and dashboards, enabling data-driven decision-making in their organizations. So, let's embark on this enriching journey and unlock the full potential of Power BI and DAX together!

CHAPTER II
Basics of DAX Language

2.1 Syntax and Basic Characteristics of DAX

In this chapter, we will dive deep into the fundamental building blocks of Data Analysis Expressions (DAX) – the syntax and basic characteristics that form the backbone of this powerful formula language. Understanding the DAX syntax is essential for creating accurate and effective calculations within Power BI.

2.1.1 DAX Formula Structure

A DAX formula is composed of functions, operators, and references to columns or measures within the data model. The formula follows a simple structure, where functions are used to perform calculations, operators connect functions and values, and references specify the data to be used in the calculation.

The basic syntax of a DAX formula is:

Result = Expression

The "Result" represents the name of the calculated column or measure, while the "Expression" is the calculation or logic written using DAX functions and operators.

2.1.2 Understanding DAX Functions

DAX offers a vast library of built-in functions that enable users to perform a wide range of calculations. Functions in DAX are similar to those found in Excel, but with some differences in behavior due to the context-aware nature of DAX. DAX functions can be categorized into several types, such as:

Aggregation functions (e.g., SUM, AVERAGE, COUNT): Perform calculations on a column or table, returning a single scalar value.

Filter functions (e.g., FILTER, ALL, TOPN): Modify the filter context of calculations, allowing users to define custom filters for data analysis.

Time intelligence functions (e.g., TOTALYTD , SAMEPERIODLASTYEAR, DATESBETWEEN): Facilitate time-based calculations, such as year-to-date totals, moving averages, and period comparisons.

Text functions (e.g., CONCATENATE, LEFT, RIGHT): Manipulate and transform text values within DAX expressions.

2.1.3 Basic Operators in DAX

DAX uses standard mathematical operators like addition (+), subtraction (-), multiplication (*), and division (/) to perform arithmetic calculations. Additionally, comparison operators (e.g., >, <, >=, <=) are used for logical evaluations in expressions.

It is crucial to understand the order of operations in DAX, similar to arithmetic operations in mathematics. Parentheses are used to control the order of evaluation when multiple operators are present in an expression.

2.1.4 Context in DAX

DAX is a context-aware language, meaning that calculations depend on the context in which they are evaluated. The context refers to the row, column, or cell context defined by filters and relationships in the data model.

Understanding context is essential for creating accurate calculations. DAX expressions can be evaluated in two primary contexts: row context and filter context. The row context is established when iterating through each row of a table, while the filter context is defined by slicers, filters, and relationships between tables.

2.1.5 DAX Data Types and Type Conversion

DAX has its own data types, including numbers, text, dates, and more. It is essential to ensure that the data types used in DAX expressions match the data types of the columns or measures they refer to. If necessary, DAX provides functions to convert data types explicitly.

In conclusion, understanding the syntax and basic characteristics of DAX is fundamental for mastering this powerful formula language. With a clear grasp of DAX functions, operators, context, and data types, users can create sophisticated calculations and unleash the full potential of Power BI for data analysis and visualization. As we progress through this chapter, we will explore practical examples and exercises to solidify our understanding of the DAX language and set the foundation for more advanced DAX techniques in the subsequent chapters. So, let's continue our journey into the world of DAX and expand our analytical prowess within Power BI!

2.2 Data Types in DAX and Data Conversion Rules

Data types play a crucial role in Data Analysis Expressions (DAX), as they define the format and behavior of values within calculations. Understanding DAX data types and the rules for data conversion is essential for ensuring accurate and consistent results in Power BI.

2.2.1 DAX Data Types

DAX supports several data types, each with specific characteristics. The primary data types in DAX are:

Numeric Data Types:

Integer (INT): Represents whole numbers without decimal points.

Decimal Number (DECIMAL): Represents numbers with decimal points, providing higher precision than the FLOAT data type.

Currency (CURRENCY): Represents monetary values with two decimal places for cents.

Text Data Type:

String (STRING): Represents text values, such as names, descriptions, or labels.

Date and Time Data Types:

Date (DATE): Represents a specific date without time information.

DateTime (DATETIME): Represents both date and time values.

Time (TIME): Represents time values without a date component.

Boolean Data Type:

Boolean (BOOLEAN): Represents true or false values.

Other Data Types:

Variant (VARIANT): A flexible data type that can hold different data types.

Binary (BINARY): Represents binary data, such as images or files.

2.2.2 Implicit and Explicit Data Conversion

DAX automatically performs data type conversions, known as implicit data conversion, when necessary. For example, if we try to add a Decimal Number to an Integer, DAX will implicitly convert the Integer to a Decimal Number to perform the addition. Implicit data conversion is convenient, but it can lead to unexpected results if not handled carefully.

In some cases, explicit data conversion may be required to ensure accurate calculations. DAX provides functions for explicit data conversion, allowing users to convert values from one data type to another explicitly. Common data conversion functions in DAX include:

CONVERT: Converts a value to a specified data type.

FORMAT: Converts a date, time, or numeric value to text using a specific format.

VALUE: Converts text to a numeric value.

2.2.3 Handling Blank and Null Values

In DAX, Blank and Null are distinct concepts. A Blank value represents the absence of a value, while a Null value indicates that a value is undefined or unknown. DAX treats Blank and Null values differently in calculations.

To handle Blank and Null values effectively, DAX provides functions such as BLANK, IFBLANK, and ISBLANK. These functions enable users to perform conditional calculations based on the presence or absence of values.

2.2.4 Data Type Conversion Errors

When performing data type conversions, it is crucial to handle potential errors gracefully. DAX provides functions like TRY, IFERROR, and ISERROR to manage data type conversion errors and avoid formula failures. By using these functions, users can create robust calculations that handle unexpected data scenarios.

2.2.5 Working with Time Zones

DAX allows users to work with time zones when dealing with date and time data. Functions like UTCNOW, UTCOFFSET, and CONVERTZONE enable users to convert date and time values to different time zones, facilitating global data analysis and reporting.

In conclusion, understanding DAX data types and data conversion rules is essential for accurate and efficient data analysis in Power BI. By mastering the concepts of implicit and explicit data conversion, handling Blank and Null values, and managing data type conversion errors, users can create robust and reliable calculations. Additionally, leveraging DAX functions for working with time zones expands the possibilities of data analysis across diverse geographical regions. As we proceed with our exploration of DAX, we will continue to explore practical examples and real-world applications, enabling you to become a proficient DAX user and enhance your data analysis capabilities in Power BI. So, let's continue our journey into the world of DAX and unlock the full potential of data analysis within Power BI!

In this section, we will delve into the practical application of DAX formulas within Power BI. Understanding how to create and use DAX formulas is essential for performing advanced calculations and unlocking the full potential of Power BI for data analysis and visualization.

2.3.1 Creating Calculated Columns

One of the primary uses of DAX formulas in Power BI is to create calculated columns. Calculated columns are new columns added to a table, and their values are derived based on DAX expressions. These expressions can involve other columns in the same table or even values from related tables.

To create a calculated column in Power BI, follow these steps:

1. Navigate to the Data view in Power BI Desktop.
2. Select the desired table, and then click on "New Column" in the Modeling tab.
3. Enter the DAX expression in the formula bar to define the calculation for the new column.

For example, to create a calculated column that calculates the total revenue, the DAX formula would be:

Total Revenue = Sales[Quantity] * Sales[UnitPrice]

The new "Total Revenue" column will automatically calculate the total revenue for each row in the Sales table based on the Quantity and UnitPrice columns.

2.3.2 Creating Measures

Measures are another vital use of DAX formulas in Power BI. Unlike calculated columns, measures are dynamic aggregations that respond to the user's interactions and the current filter context. Measures are typically used for calculations such as totals, averages, and percentages.

To create a measure in Power BI, follow these steps:

1. Navigate to the Data view in Power BI Desktop.
2. Select the desired table, and then click on "New Measure" in the Modeling tab.
3. Enter the DAX expression in the formula bar to define the calculation for the measure.

For example, to create a measure that calculates the total sales amount, the DAX formula would be:

Total Sales = SUM(Sales[SalesAmount])

The "Total Sales" measure will provide the sum of the SalesAmount column based on the current filter context in the report or visualization.

2.3.3 Using DAX in Visualizations

DAX formulas are not limited to calculated columns and measures; they can also be used directly within visualizations. Power BI allows users to create custom calculations in visualizations using DAX expressions, providing more flexibility and analytical capabilities.

For instance, in a line chart showing sales trends over time, you might want to add a trendline that represents a moving average. To achieve this, you can create a new DAX measure that calculates the moving average and then use this measure in the line chart visualization.

2.3.4 Iterating Functions in DAX

DAX provides iterating functions that allow users to perform calculations over multiple rows or tables. These functions, such as SUMX, AVERAGEX, and COUNTX, iterate through each row or table and perform the calculation defined in the DAX expression.

Iterating functions are particularly useful when performing calculations involving related tables or when custom aggregations are required.

2.3.5 Debugging DAX Formulas

As DAX formulas become more complex, it is essential to know how to debug and troubleshoot errors. Power BI provides features like the "Evaluate" and "Expression Error" dialogs, which help users analyze and understand how DAX expressions are evaluated step-by-step.

The "Evaluate" dialog displays the intermediate results of a DAX expression, making it easier to identify issues and verify the correctness of the calculation.

In conclusion, using DAX formulas in Power BI opens up a world of possibilities for advanced data analysis and visualization. By creating calculated columns and measures, utilizing DAX in visualizations, and leveraging iterating functions, users can perform complex calculations and derive meaningful insights from their data. Additionally, understanding how to debug DAX formulas ensures accurate and reliable results in Power BI reports and dashboards. As we progress in our exploration of DAX, we will continue to explore more advanced DAX functions and techniques, further enhancing your analytical capabilities within Power BI. So, let's continue our journey into the world of DAX and unleash the true power of data analysis and visualization!

CHAPTER III
Basic DAX Functions

3.1 SUM, AVERAGE, MIN, and MAX Functions - Calculating Total, Average, Minimum, and Maximum Values

In this chapter, we will explore some of the most fundamental and widely used DAX functions: SUM, AVERAGE, MIN, and MAX. These functions are essential for performing basic calculations on numeric data within Power BI and are the building blocks of more complex analyses.

3.1.1 SUM Function

The SUM function in DAX is used to calculate the total sum of numeric values in a column. It is particularly useful when working with data that requires aggregation, such as sales revenue, quantities, or expenses.

The syntax of the SUM function is straightforward:

SUM(<column>)

Here, `<column>` represents the column from which you want to calculate the sum.

For example, let's say we have a Sales table with a SalesAmount column. To calculate the total sales amount, we can use the SUM function as follows:

Total Sales = SUM(Sales[SalesAmount])

The "Total Sales" measure will provide the sum of all values in the SalesAmount column, giving us the total sales amount.

3.1.2 AVERAGE Function

The AVERAGE function in DAX calculates the arithmetic mean of numeric values in a column. It provides the average value, which is the sum of all values divided by the number of values in the column.

The syntax of the AVERAGE function is similar to the SUM function:

AVERAGE(<column>)

By applying the AVERAGE function to a column, we can obtain the average value.

For example, using the same Sales table, we can calculate the average sales amount as follows:

Average Sales = AVERAGE(Sales[SalesAmount])

The "Average Sales" measure will provide the average value of all the sales amounts in the SalesAmount column.

3.1.3 MIN Function

The MIN function in DAX is used to find the minimum value in a column of numeric data. It helps identify the smallest value within the dataset.

The syntax of the MIN function is as follows:

MIN(<column>)

By applying the MIN function to a column, we can determine the minimum value.

For instance, if we want to find the minimum sales amount in the Sales table, we can use the MIN function:

Minimum Sales Amount = MIN(Sales[SalesAmount])

The "Minimum Sales Amount" measure will provide the smallest value in the SalesAmount column, indicating the minimum sales amount.

3.1.4 MAX Function

On the other hand, the MAX function in DAX is used to find the maximum value in a column of numeric data. It helps identify the largest value within the dataset.

The syntax of the MAX function is similar to the MIN function:

MAX(<column>)

By applying the MAX function to a column, we can determine the maximum value.

Continuing with our Sales table example, let's calculate the maximum sales amount using the MAX function:

Maximum Sales Amount = MAX(Sales[SalesAmount])

The "Maximum Sales Amount" measure will provide the largest value in the SalesAmount column, representing the maximum sales amount.

3.1.5 Using Functions in Calculated Columns and Measures

The SUM, AVERAGE, MIN, and MAX functions are versatile and can be used in both calculated columns and measures. In calculated columns, these functions help create new columns that store aggregated or calculated values based on the data in other columns. In measures, they provide dynamic aggregations that respond to the current filter context and user interactions.

For instance, in addition to creating measures for total sales, average sales, minimum sales amount, and maximum sales amount, we can also create calculated columns that store these values for each row in the Sales table. This allows us to visualize and analyze individual sales records in the context of the overall data.

3.1.6 Handling Non-Numeric Values

It is essential to consider that the SUM, AVERAGE, MIN, and MAX functions in DAX only work with numeric data types. If a column contains non-numeric values, these functions will return errors or incorrect results. Therefore, it is crucial to ensure that the data in the column is of the correct data type for the functions to work accurately.

In conclusion, the SUM, AVERAGE, MIN, and MAX functions are fundamental DAX functions that perform basic calculations on numeric data in Power BI. By leveraging these functions in calculated columns and measures, users can calculate total sums, averages, minimum, and maximum values for various metrics. Understanding how to handle numeric data effectively and use these functions correctly is essential for accurate data analysis and visualization within Power BI. As we continue our exploration of DAX in subsequent chapters, we will discover more advanced DAX functions and techniques to enhance our analytical capabilities further. So, let's continue our journey into the world of DAX and unlock the full potential of data analysis and visualization within Power BI!

3.2 COUNT and COUNTA Functions - Counting Rows and Non-Empty Values

In this section, we will explore two essential DAX functions: COUNT and COUNTA. These functions play a crucial role in data analysis as they enable users to count the number of rows and non-empty values within a column or table in Power BI.

3.2.1 COUNT Function

The COUNT function in DAX is used to count the number of rows in a column that contain numeric values. It provides a simple and effective way to calculate the cardinality of a column, which is the number of unique values present.

The syntax of the COUNT function is as follows:

COUNT(<column>)

Here, `<column>` represents the column for which you want to count the numeric values.

For example, consider a Sales table with a Quantity column. To count the number of sales transactions, we can use the COUNT function as follows:

Number of Sales = COUNT(Sales[Quantity])

The "Number of Sales" measure will provide the count of rows in the Quantity column that contain numeric values, representing the number of sales transactions.

3.2.2 COUNTA Function

While the COUNT function counts only numeric values, the COUNTA function in DAX goes a step further by counting all non-empty values within a column or table, regardless of data type. This makes it particularly useful for columns that contain a mix of data types, including text, numbers, and dates.

The syntax of the COUNTA function is similar to the COUNT function:

COUNTA(<column>)

By applying the COUNTA function to a column, we can determine the count of non-empty values.

For instance, let's consider a Customer table with a City column that contains the names of cities where customers are located. To count the number of customers for whom the city information is available, we can use the COUNTA function:

Number of Customers with City Info = COUNTA(Customer[City])

The "Number of Customers with City Info" measure will provide the count of non-empty cells in the City column, indicating the number of customers with available city information.

3.2.3 Distinction between COUNT and COUNTA

It is essential to note the difference between the COUNT and COUNTA functions. While both functions provide counts, the COUNT function only works with numeric values, while the COUNTA function considers all non-empty values, regardless of data type.

If you use the COUNT function on a column that contains non-numeric values, it will return 0. On the other hand, the COUNTA function will return the count of non-empty values, even if they are non-numeric.

For example, if we have a Product table with a Category column containing categories of products, using COUNT on the Category column will yield 0, as categories are non-numeric values. However, using COUNTA will return the count of non-empty cells, giving us the total number of products with assigned categories.

3.2.4 COUNTROWS Function

In addition to COUNT and COUNTA, there is another useful function in DAX called COUNTROWS. The COUNTROWS function is used to count the number of rows in a table or a table expression.

The syntax of the COUNTROWS function is as follows:

COUNTROWS(<table>)

Here, `<table>` represents the table for which you want to count the rows.

For example, suppose we have a Customer table. To count the total number of customers, we can use the COUNTROWS function as follows:

Total Customers = COUNTROWS(Customer)

The "Total Customers" measure will provide the count of all rows in the Customer table, representing the total number of customers.

3.2.5 Using COUNT and COUNTA in Measures

Similar to other DAX functions, COUNT and COUNTA can be used to create calculated columns and measures. Calculated columns can be useful for calculating counts that remain static for each row in a table. On the other hand, measures offer dynamic counts that respond to user interactions and the current filter context.

3.2.6 Dealing with Blank Values

When using the COUNT and COUNTA functions, it is essential to consider how they handle blank values. The COUNT function treats blank values as 0, meaning it will not count them as part of the result. In contrast, the COUNTA function includes blank values in the count, as they are considered non-empty.

To exclude blank values from the count, users can filter or manipulate the data appropriately, or use additional functions like FILTER or IF to control the count more precisely.

In conclusion, the COUNT and COUNTA functions are invaluable tools in DAX for counting rows and non-empty values within a column or table. By leveraging these functions in calculated columns and measures, users can obtain the cardinality of columns, count the occurrences of specific values, and calculate dynamic counts based on the current filter context. Understanding the distinction between COUNT and COUNTA and how to handle blank values ensures accurate and reliable results in data analysis. As we continue our journey into the world of DAX, we will explore more advanced DAX functions and techniques to enhance our analytical capabilities further. So, let's continue our exploration and unlock the full potential of data analysis and visualization within Power BI!

3.3 IF and SWITCH Functions - Handling Conditions and Replacing Values

In this section, we will explore two powerful DAX functions: IF and SWITCH. These functions are essential for handling conditions and replacing values within Power BI calculations, enabling users to perform dynamic transformations based on specific criteria.

3.3.1 IF Function

The IF function in DAX is used to evaluate a condition and return different results based on whether the condition is true or false. It allows users to create conditional expressions, making it a versatile tool for data analysis.

The syntax of the IF function is as follows:

IF(<condition>, <value_if_true>, <value_if_false>)

Here, <condition> represents the logical test or condition to be evaluated. If the condition is true, the function returns <value_if_true>, and if the condition is false, it returns <value_if_false>.

For example, consider a Sales table with a Quantity column. To create a measure that categorizes sales transactions as "High" or "Low" based on a threshold value, we can use the IF function as follows:

Sales Category = IF(Sales[Quantity] > 100, "High", "Low")

The "Sales Category" measure will evaluate whether the quantity of each transaction is greater than 100. If it is true, the measure returns "High," indicating a high-sales transaction. Otherwise, it returns "Low," indicating a low-sales transaction.

3.3.2 Nested IF Statements

The IF function can also be nested, meaning that the value_if_true or value_if_false arguments can be additional IF functions. This enables users to create more complex conditions and multiple branches of logic.

For instance, suppose we want to categorize sales transactions into three categories: "High," "Medium," and "Low," based on different quantity thresholds. We can achieve this with nested IF statements:

Sales Category = IF(Sales[Quantity] > 200, "High", IF(Sales[Quantity] > 100, "Medium", "Low"))

The "Sales Category" measure will first check if the quantity is greater than 200. If true, it returns "High." If false, it checks if the quantity is greater than 100. If true, it returns "Medium." Otherwise, it returns "Low."

3.3.3 SWITCH Function

The SWITCH function in DAX provides an alternative approach to handling multiple conditions. It is especially useful when dealing with a large number of conditions or when the conditions are based on specific values.

The syntax of the SWITCH function is as follows:

SWITCH(<expression>, <value1>, <result1>, <value2>, <result2>, ..., <default_result>)

Here, <expression> represents the value to be evaluated. The function then compares <expression> to the provided <value> arguments. If a match is found, it returns the corresponding <result>. If no match is found, it returns the <default_result>.

For example, consider a Product table with a Category column. To create a measure that groups products into different departments based on their category, we can use the SWITCH function as follows:

Department = SWITCH(Product[Category], "Electronics", "Tech", "Clothing", "Apparel", "Home", "Houseware", "Other")

The "Department" measure will evaluate the value in the Category column and return the corresponding department name based on the SWITCH conditions.

3.3.4 Handling Error Conditions with IF and SWITCH

Both the IF and SWITCH functions can be used to handle error conditions and display specific values when an error occurs. For instance, suppose we have a Sales table with a UnitPrice column that may contain negative values due to data entry errors. To handle these errors and replace negative values with zero, we can use the IF function:

Adjusted Unit Price = IF(Sales[UnitPrice] < 0, 0, Sales[UnitPrice])

The "Adjusted Unit Price" measure will check if the UnitPrice is less than zero. If true, it returns 0; otherwise, it returns the original UnitPrice value.

Similarly, the SWITCH function can be used to handle error conditions by providing a default result when no match is found. This ensures that unexpected or missing values are handled gracefully in calculations.

3.3.5 Using Functions in Calculated Columns and Measures

Both the IF and SWITCH functions are versatile and can be used in both calculated columns and measures. Calculated columns can be helpful when you want to create new columns based on specific conditions that remain static for each row. On the other hand, measures offer dynamic calculations that respond to the current filter context and user interactions.

3.3.6 Advanced Logic with IF and SWITCH

The IF and SWITCH functions can be combined with other DAX functions and expressions to create even more sophisticated logic. By nesting multiple IF or SWITCH statements and using other DAX functions like AND, OR, and NOT, users can build complex calculations and derive meaningful insights from their data.

In conclusion, the IF and SWITCH functions are powerful tools in DAX for handling conditions and replacing values in Power BI calculations. By using the IF function, users can create simple or nested conditional expressions to perform dynamic transformations based on specific criteria. The SWITCH function offers an efficient and concise way to handle multiple conditions and provide results for different cases. Leveraging these functions in calculated columns and measures empowers users to perform advanced data analysis and ensure data integrity by handling error conditions. As we continue our exploration of DAX in subsequent chapters, we will discover more advanced DAX functions and techniques to enhance our analytical capabilities further. So, let's continue our journey into the world of DAX and unlock the full potential of data analysis and visualization within Power BI!

CHAPTER IV
Calculating Strings and Text with DAX

4.1 CONCATENATE Function - Combining Text Strings

In this chapter, we will explore the CONCATENATE function in DAX, which is a powerful tool for combining text strings in Power BI. Concatenation allows users to merge text values from different columns or add custom text to create informative and structured narratives in reports and visualizations.

4.1.1 Understanding Concatenation

Concatenation is the process of joining multiple text strings together to form a single text string. It is a common operation in data analysis when we want to create meaningful labels, titles, or descriptions that involve multiple text elements.

For example, consider a Sales table with columns for "Product Name," "Brand," and "Category." To create a concise product label that includes all this information, we can use concatenation to combine these text strings into one:

Product Label = CONCATENATE(Sales[Product Name], " - ", Sales[Brand], " - ", Sales[Category])

The "Product Label" column will display a text string that combines the "Product Name," "Brand," and "Category" with hyphens as separators.

4.1.2 The CONCATENATE Function

The CONCATENATE function in DAX is used to concatenate two or more text strings. It takes multiple arguments, each representing a text string, and combines them in the order they are provided.

The syntax of the CONCATENATE function is as follows:

CONCATENATE(<text1>, <text2>, ..., <textN>)

Here, `<text1>, <text2>, ..., <textN>` are the text strings to be concatenated. They can be column references, text enclosed in double quotes, or other DAX expressions that result in text values.

4.1.3 Handling Blank and Null Values

When using the CONCATENATE function, it is essential to consider how it handles blank and null values. If any of the arguments provided to CONCATENATE are blank or null, the resulting concatenation will also contain a blank value.

To handle blank or null values effectively, users can use the IF or IFERROR functions to replace them with custom text or empty strings before performing the concatenation.

For instance, let's say we want to create a custom sales description that includes the "Product Name," "Brand," and "Category." However, some products may not have a specific brand or category, resulting in blank values. We can handle this scenario as follows:

Sales Description =

CONCATENATE(

   Sales[Product Name],

   IF(NOT(ISBLANK(Sales[Brand])), CONCATENATE(" - ", Sales[Brand]), ""),

   IF(NOT(ISBLANK(Sales[Category])), CONCATENATE(" - ", Sales[Category]), "")

)

In this example, if the "Brand" or "Category" is blank, the corresponding part of the description will be omitted, preventing unnecessary hyphens in the result.

4.1.4 Using Ampersand Operator as a Shortcut

While the CONCATENATE function is a powerful tool for text concatenation, DAX also provides a shortcut using the ampersand (&) operator. The ampersand operator performs the same task as CONCATENATE but with a more concise syntax.

The syntax of the ampersand operator is as follows:

<text1> & <text2> & ... & <textN>

Using the ampersand operator, the previous example can be written as follows:

Sales Description =

Sales[Product Name] &

IF(NOT(ISBLANK(Sales[Brand])), CONCATENATE(" - ", Sales[Brand]), "") &

IF(NOT(ISBLANK(Sales[Category])), CONCATENATE(" - ", Sales[Category]), "")

Both CONCATENATE and the ampersand operator achieve the same result. Users can choose the one that suits their preference and readability of the formula.

4.1.5 Converting Numbers and Dates to Text

When concatenating numbers or dates with text strings, it is essential to consider their data types. DAX requires that all values being concatenated have the same data type. Therefore, if a number or date needs to be included in a text concatenation, it must be converted to text using the FORMAT function.

For example, suppose we want to create a label that displays the order date along with the order number. We can use the FORMAT function to convert the date to text before concatenating it with the order number:

Order Label = CONCATENATE("Order #", Sales[Order Number], " - ", FORMAT(Sales[Order Date], "yyyy-mm-dd"))

The "Order Label" column will display a text string that includes the order number preceded by "Order #" and the formatted order date.

4.1.6 Concatenating with Line Breaks

In some cases, users may want to concatenate text strings with line breaks to display them as separate lines in a visual or report. To achieve this, DAX provides the UNICHAR function, which allows users to include special characters like line breaks in their concatenation.

For instance, let's say we have a Product table with columns for "Product Name," "Description," and "Price."

4.2 LEFT, RIGHT, and MID Functions - Extracting Parts of a String

In this section, we will explore three useful DAX functions: LEFT, RIGHT, and MID. These functions allow users to extract specific parts of a text string in Power BI. Whether it's extracting the first few characters, the last few characters, or a substring from the middle, these functions provide flexibility in handling text data.

4.2.1 Understanding String Extraction

String extraction is the process of retrieving a portion of a text string based on specified criteria. This can be helpful when working with text data that contains relevant information within a larger string.

For example, consider a Product table with a "Product Code" column. To extract the product category code from the full product code, we can use the LEFT or RIGHT functions to capture the desired part of the string.

4.2.2 LEFT Function

The LEFT function in DAX is used to extract a specified number of characters from the beginning of a text string. It takes two arguments: the text string and the number of characters to extract.

The syntax of the LEFT function is as follows:

LEFT(<text>, <num_chars>)

Here, `<text>` represents the text string from which characters will be extracted, and `<num_chars>` represents the number of characters to be extracted from the left.

For example, let's consider a Product table with a "Product Code" column containing alphanumeric codes. To extract the first three characters (the category code) from the product code, we can use the LEFT function:

Category Code = LEFT(Product[Product Code], 3)

The "Category Code" column will display the first three characters of the "Product Code," representing the category code.

4.2.3 RIGHT Function

Similar to the LEFT function, the RIGHT function is used to extract a specified number of characters, but from the end of a text string. It also takes two arguments: the text string and the number of characters to extract.

The syntax of the RIGHT function is as follows:

RIGHT(<text>, <num_chars>)

Here, `<text>` represents the text string from which characters will be extracted, and `<num_chars>` represents the number of characters to be extracted from the right.

For example, using the same Product table, if we want to extract the last four characters (the product ID) from the product code, we can use the RIGHT function:

Product ID = RIGHT(Product[Product Code], 4)

The "Product ID" column will display the last four characters of the "Product Code," representing the product ID.

4.2.4 MID Function

The MID function in DAX is used to extract a substring from the middle of a text string. It takes three arguments: the text string, the starting position of the substring, and the number of characters to be extracted.

The syntax of the MID function is as follows:

MID(<text>, <start_pos>, <num_chars>)

Here, `<text>` represents the text string from which the substring will be extracted, `<start_pos>` represents the starting position of the substring, and `<num_chars>` represents the number of characters to be extracted.

For example, let's consider a Sales table with a "Customer Name" column containing the full names of customers. To extract the first name from the "Customer Name," we can use the MID function along with the FIND function to determine the starting position:

First Name =

MID(

   Sales[Customer Name],

   1,

   FIND(" ", Sales[Customer Name]) - 1

)

The "First Name" column will display the first name of each customer by extracting the substring from the beginning of the "Customer Name" until the space character.

4.2.5 Handling Variable-Length Substrings

When using the MID function to extract a substring from the middle of a text string, it is important to consider that the substring length may vary based on specific conditions. In such cases, users can use additional DAX functions and expressions to determine the appropriate length dynamically.

For example, consider a Product table with a "Product Description" column. The length of the product description may vary, and we want to extract the first 30 characters for a concise display. We can achieve this as follows:

Short Description =

IF(

   LEN(Product[Product Description]) <= 30,

   Product[Product Description],

   MID(Product[Product Description], 1, 30) & "..."

)

In this example, if the length of the product description is 30 characters or less, the "Short Description" column will display the full description. If the description is longer than 30 characters, it will extract the first 30 characters and append "..." to indicate that it has been truncated.

4.2.6 Using Functions in Calculated Columns and Measures

The LEFT, RIGHT, and MID functions can be used in both calculated columns and measures. Calculated columns are useful when you want to extract parts of text strings that remain constant for each row. On the other hand, measures offer dynamic extractions that respond to the current filter context and user interactions.

4.2.7 Additional Considerations

When extracting substrings, it is essential to handle cases where the starting position or number of characters to extract may result in errors due to invalid arguments. Users can use the IFERROR function to handle potential errors gracefully and provide fallback values or error messages when necessary.

In conclusion, the LEFT, RIGHT, and MID functions are valuable tools in DAX for extracting specific parts of text strings in Power BI. Whether it's retrieving characters from the beginning, end, or middle of a string, these functions provide flexibility in handling text data. By combining these functions with other DAX expressions, users can create calculated columns and measures that extract variable-length substrings based on specific conditions. Understanding how to handle varying substring lengths and potential errors ensures accurate and reliable results in data analysis. As we continue our exploration of DAX in subsequent chapters, we will discover more advanced DAX functions and techniques to enhance our analytical capabilities further. So, let's continue our journey into the world of DAX and unlock the full potential of data analysis and visualization within Power BI!

In this section, we will explore the LEN function in DAX, which is a simple yet powerful tool for counting the number of characters in a text string. The LEN function plays a crucial role in various data analysis scenarios, from checking data quality to creating dynamic calculations based on text length.

4.3.1 Understanding the LEN Function

The LEN function in DAX is used to return the number of characters in a given text string. It is particularly useful when dealing with text data, as it provides valuable information about the length of strings.

The syntax of the LEN function is as follows:

LEN(<text>)

Here, `<text>` represents the text string for which you want to count the number of characters.

For example, consider a Sales table with a "Product Name" column. To determine the length of each product name, we can use the LEN function as follows:

Product Name Length = LEN(Sales[Product Name])

The "Product Name Length" column will display the number of characters in each product name.

4.3.2 Handling Blank and Null Values

When using the LEN function, it is important to consider how it handles blank and null values. If the provided text argument is blank or null, the LEN function will return 0.

To handle blank or null values effectively, users can use the IF or IFERROR functions to replace them with custom text or other expressions before applying the LEN function.

For instance, let's say we want to calculate the length of product descriptions in the Product table. Some products may have missing descriptions, resulting in blank values. We can handle this scenario as follows:

Description Length = IF(ISBLANK(Product[Description]), 0, LEN(Product[Description]))

In this example, if the "Description" is blank, the "Description Length" column will display 0. Otherwise, it will calculate the length of the description using the LEN function.

4.3.3 Use Case: Checking Data Quality

The LEN function is an essential tool for checking data quality, especially when dealing with text data. By calculating the length of text strings in a column, users can identify anomalies, such as overly short or unusually long values, which may indicate data entry errors or inconsistencies.

For example, in a Customer table, suppose we have a "Username" column for customer account names. To ensure data quality, we can create a measure that checks the length of usernames to detect any unusually short or long names:

Data Quality Check =

IF(LEN(Customer[Username]) < 4 || LEN(Customer[Username]) > 20, "Data Issue", "Data OK")

The "Data Quality Check" measure will flag any usernames that have fewer than four characters or more than twenty characters as "Data Issue," indicating a potential data quality problem.

4.3.4 Use Case: Dynamic Formatting and Labeling

The LEN function can also be used to dynamically format data or generate labels based on text length. By evaluating the length of a text string in a measure, users can create dynamic visualizations or apply conditional formatting to highlight specific data patterns.

For example, consider a Sales table with a "Customer Name" column. To create a dynamic visualization that changes the font color based on the length of customer names, we can use the LEN function along with conditional formatting rules:

Font Color =

IF(

   LEN(Sales[Customer Name]) <= 10, "Green",

   IF(LEN(Sales[Customer Name]) > 10 && LEN(Sales[Customer Name]) <= 15, "Orange", "Red")

)

In this example, if the length of the "Customer Name" is ten characters or less, the font color will be green. If it is between eleven and fifteen characters, the font color will be orange. For names longer than fifteen characters, the font color will be red.

4.3.5 Use Case: Truncating Text for Display

Another practical use of the LEN function is truncating text for display purposes, such as in tables or visualizations with limited space. By checking the length of text strings and using the LEFT or RIGHT functions, users can create concise and visually appealing displays.

For instance, suppose we want to display product names in a table with a maximum width of 20 characters. We can create a calculated column to truncate product names exceeding this length:

Truncated Name =

IF(LEN(Product[Product Name]) > 20, LEFT(Product[Product Name], 17) & "...", Product[Product Name])

The "Truncated Name" column will display the first 17 characters of the product name, followed by "..." if the name exceeds 20 characters.

4.3.6 Using the LEN Function in Calculations

The LEN function is commonly used in calculated columns, measures, and calculated tables. Its ability to calculate the length of text strings based on specific conditions makes it a valuable asset in data analysis and reporting.

4.3.7 Additional Considerations

When using the LEN function, it is essential to consider the language settings in Power BI, as some languages may treat certain characters as multiple characters, impacting the result of the LEN function. For instance, accented characters or emojis may have varying lengths in different languages.

In conclusion, the LEN function is a valuable tool in DAX for counting characters in text strings within Power BI. Its simplicity and versatility make it a fundamental function for various data analysis tasks, such as checking data quality, generating dynamic formatting and labels, and truncating text for display. By incorporating the LEN function into calculated columns and measures, users can gain valuable insights into text data and enhance data visualizations and reporting. As we continue our exploration of DAX in subsequent chapters, we will discover more advanced DAX functions and techniques to further enhance our analytical capabilities. So, let's continue our journey into the world of DAX and unlock the full potential of data analysis and visualization within Power BI!

CHAPTER V
Calculating Time and Dates with DAX

5.1. DATE and TIME functions - Creating date and time values

In this chapter, we will delve into the DATE and TIME functions in DAX, which are essential for working with date and time data in Power BI. These functions enable users to create date and time values, which are fundamental for time-based analysis, trend identification, and time intelligence calculations.

5.1.1 Understanding Date and Time in DAX

Date and time data are common types of information in datasets, and analyzing them is crucial for understanding trends, seasonality, and performance over time. In Power BI, date and time values can be represented as separate columns or combined into a single DateTime column.

The DATE and TIME functions in DAX are used to create date and time values, respectively. These functions are especially useful when creating calculated columns, measures, or performing time-related calculations.

5.1.2 The DATE Function

The DATE function in DAX is used to construct a date value from individual components, such as year, month, and day. It takes three arguments: the year, month, and day integers.

The syntax of the DATE function is as follows:

```
DATE(<year>, <month>, <day>)
```

Here, `<year>` represents the year as a four-digit integer, `<month>` represents the month as a one or two-digit integer (1 to 12), and `<day>` represents the day of the month as a one or two-digit integer (1 to 31).

For example, to create a date value for January 1, 2023, we can use the DATE function as follows:

```
Start Date = DATE(2023, 1, 1)
```

The "Start Date" column will display January 1, 2023, as a date value.

5.1.3 The TIME Function

The TIME function in DAX is used to construct a time value from individual components, such as hours, minutes, and seconds. It takes three arguments: the hour, minute, and second integers.

The syntax of the TIME function is as follows:

```
TIME(<hour>, <minute>, <second>)
```

Here, `<hour>` represents the hour as an integer (0 to 23), `<minute>` represents the minute as an integer (0 to 59), and `<second>` represents the second as an integer (0 to 59).

For example, to create a time value for 3:30:00 PM, we can use the TIME function as follows:

```
Time of Day = TIME(15, 30, 0)
```

The "Time of Day" column will display 3:30:00 PM as a time value.

5.1.4 Combining DATE and TIME Functions

To create a DateTime value that includes both date and time components, users can combine the DATE and TIME functions. This is particularly useful when dealing with time-based events or capturing timestamps.

For example, suppose we have a Sales table with separate columns for "Date" and "Time." To combine these into a DateTime column, we can use the DATE and TIME functions as follows:

```
DateTime Stamp = DATE(Sales[Year], Sales[Month], Sales[Day]) + TIME(Sales[Hour],
Sales[Minute], Sales[Second])
```

The "DateTime Stamp" column will display a single DateTime value that includes both the date
and time components.

5.1.5 Working with Textual Dates and Times

In some datasets, dates and times may be represented as text strings instead of separate columns
or DateTime values. In such cases, users can convert textual dates and times to DateTime values
using the DATEVALUE and TIMEVALUE functions, respectively.

For example, suppose we have a "Date Text" column containing date values in the format
"YYYY-MM-DD." To convert these text values into DateTime values, we can use the
DATEVALUE function:

```
Date as DateTime = DATEVALUE(Sales[Date Text])
```

The "Date as DateTime" column will display the date values from the "Date Text" column as
DateTime values.

Similarly, if we have a "Time Text" column containing time values in the format "HH:MM:SS,"
we can convert them to DateTime values using the TIMEVALUE function:

```
Time as DateTime = TIMEVALUE(Sales[Time Text])
```

The "Time as DateTime" column will display the time values from the "Time Text" column as DateTime values.

5.1.6 Handling Date and Time Calculations

Once date and time values are created or converted, users can perform various time-related calculations using DAX. These calculations include calculating the difference between dates, extracting components like day of the week or month, and comparing date and time values.

For instance, to calculate the number of days between two dates, we can use the DATEDIFF function:

```
Days Between = DATEDIFF(Sales[Start Date], Sales[End Date], DAY)
```

The "Days Between" measure will calculate the number of days between the "Start Date" and "End Date" columns.

Similarly, to extract the month component from a date value, we can use the MONTH function:

```
Month Number = MONTH(Sales[Date])
```

The "Month Number" column will display the month component (1 to 12) of the date in the "Date" column.

5.1.7 Time Intelligence with DAX

Date and time functions are fundamental for time intelligence calculations, such as year-to-date (YTD), month-to-date (MTD), and same period last year (SPLY) calculations. These calculations are crucial for trend analysis, comparing performance over time, and identifying seasonality patterns.

DAX provides a set of time intelligence functions, such as TOTALYTD, TOTALMTD, and SAMEPERIODLASTYEAR, to simplify these calculations. These functions leverage the inherent time intelligence capabilities of Power BI, considering filters, relationships, and date hierarchies.

For example, to calculate year-to-date sales, we can use the TOTALYTD function:

```
YTD Sales = TOTALYTD(SUM(Sales[Revenue]), Sales[Date])
```

The "YTD Sales" measure will display the total revenue from the beginning of the year up to the current date, considering any filters applied to the report.

5.1.8 Using Functions in Calculated Columns and Measures

Both the DATE and TIME functions, along with other date and time intelligence functions, can be used in calculated columns, measures, and calculated tables. Their versatility and ease of use make them essential tools for time-based analysis and reporting in Power BI.

5.1.9 Additional Considerations

When working with dates and times, it is crucial to ensure that date columns are marked as date data types in Power BI. This enables the built-in time intelligence capabilities and ensures accurate date-based calculations.

Additionally, users should be mindful of any potential data inconsistencies or missing values in date and time columns, as they may impact the results of time-related calculations.

In conclusion, the DATE and TIME functions in DAX are fundamental for working with date and time data in Power BI. They allow users to create date and time values, combine them into DateTime values, and perform various time-related calculations. When used in combination with time intelligence functions, they provide a powerful toolkit for time-based analysis, trend identification, and performance comparisons over time. As we continue our exploration of DAX in subsequent chapters, we will discover more advanced date and time functions and techniques to further enhance our time-based analyses and gain deeper insights from our data. So, let's continue our journey into the world of DAX and unlock the full potential of time-based analytics within Power BI!

5.2 DATEDIFF and DATEADD Functions - Calculating Time Spans and Adding/Subtracting Time Intervals

In this section, we will explore the DATEDIFF and DATEADD functions in DAX, which are essential tools for performing time-based calculations in Power BI. These functions enable users to calculate time spans between two dates and add or subtract time intervals from a given date, respectively.

5.2.1 Understanding Time-Based Calculations

Time-based calculations are common in data analysis, especially when working with date and time data. Whether it's calculating the age of customers, measuring the duration between two events, or forecasting future dates, DATEDIFF and DATEADD are versatile functions that empower users to perform various time-related calculations.

5.2.2 The DATEDIFF Function

The DATEDIFF function in DAX is used to calculate the difference between two dates in terms of a specified time unit. It takes three arguments: the start date, end date, and the time unit for which the difference will be calculated.

The syntax of the DATEDIFF function is as follows:

```
DATEDIFF(<start_date>, <end_date>, <time_unit>)
```

Here, `<start_date>` and `<end_date>` are the two dates between which the difference will be calculated, and `<time_unit>` is the time unit in which the difference will be expressed.

For example, let's consider a Sales table with a "Order Date" and a "Delivery Date" column. To calculate the number of days it took to deliver each order, we can use the DATEDIFF function as follows:

```

Delivery Duration (Days) = DATEDIFF(Sales[Order Date], Sales[Delivery Date], DAY)

```

The "Delivery Duration (Days)" column will display the number of days it took for each order to be delivered.

5.2.3 Available Time Units for DATEDIFF

The DATEDIFF function supports various time units that users can choose based on their specific analysis requirements. Some of the commonly used time units include:

- YEAR: Calculate the difference in years between two dates.

- QUARTER: Calculate the difference in quarters between two dates.

- MONTH: Calculate the difference in months between two dates.

- DAY: Calculate the difference in days between two dates.

- HOUR: Calculate the difference in hours between two dates.

- MINUTE: Calculate the difference in minutes between two dates.

- SECOND: Calculate the difference in seconds between two dates.

Users should select the appropriate time unit that best aligns with the nature of their data and the insights they seek to gain.

5.2.4 The DATEADD Function

The DATEADD function in DAX is used to add or subtract a specific time interval from a given date. It takes three arguments: the base date, the number of time units to add or subtract, and the time unit itself.

The syntax of the DATEADD function is as follows:

```
DATEADD(<base_date>, <number_of_units>, <time_unit>)
```

Here, `<base_date>` is the date to which the time interval will be added or subtracted, `<number_of_units>` is the number of time units to adjust, and `<time_unit>` is the time unit to be used for the adjustment.

For example, suppose we have a "Start Date" column in a Project table and want to calculate the project's end date by adding six months to the start date. We can use the DATEADD function as follows:

```
End Date = DATEADD(Project[Start Date], 6, MONTH)
```

The "End Date" column will display the date that is six months after the "Start Date."

5.2.5 Available Time Units for DATEADD

The DATEADD function supports the same time units as the DATEDIFF function, allowing users to precisely adjust dates based on their analysis requirements. By using different time units, users can perform diverse time-based calculations and create dynamic analyses that respond to changing data.

5.2.6 Handling Date and Time Calculations with DATEADD and DATEDIFF

The combination of the DATEADD and DATEDIFF functions enables users to perform sophisticated time-based calculations in Power BI. For instance, consider a Sales table with a "Transaction Date" column. We can create a measure to calculate the number of days since the last transaction using both functions:

```
Days Since Last Transaction =
DATEDIFF(
    MAX(Sales[Transaction Date]),
    TODAY(),
    DAY
)
```

In this example, the "Days Since Last Transaction" measure will calculate the difference in days between the maximum transaction date in the Sales table and the current date (TODAY).

5.2.7 Handling Future and Past Dates

When using the DATEADD function to calculate future or past dates, it is essential to consider potential data inconsistencies or illogical results. For instance, adding a negative number of units to a base date may result in dates that do not make sense in the context of the data.

To ensure that date calculations are accurate and meaningful, users should apply appropriate filtering or use conditional statements to handle future or past date scenarios. Additionally, it is advisable to check for any data anomalies that may impact the results of time-based calculations.

5.2.8 Using Functions in Calculated Columns and Measures

Both the DATEDIFF and DATEADD functions, along with other time intelligence functions, can be used in calculated columns, measures, and calculated tables. Their flexibility and ability to respond dynamically to data make them valuable assets in time-based analysis and reporting.

5.2.9 Additional Considerations

When working with dates and time intervals, users should ensure that date columns are marked as date data types in Power BI. This enables the built-in time intelligence capabilities and ensures accurate time-based calculations.

Furthermore, it is essential to consider the time zone settings in Power BI, especially when dealing with global data. Users should be mindful of potential discrepancies that may arise from time zone conversions, especially when working with real-time data or data from different regions.

In conclusion, the DATEDIFF and DATEADD functions are essential tools in DAX for performing time-based calculations in Power BI. The DATEDIFF function allows users to calculate time spans between two dates, while the DATEADD function enables the addition or subtraction of time intervals to or from a given date. By combining these functions with time intelligence functions and other DAX expressions, users can create powerful time-based analyses, gain deeper insights from their data, and make data-driven decisions. As we continue our exploration of DAX in subsequent chapters, we will discover more advanced date and time functions and techniques to further enhance our time-based analytics and unlock the full potential of time-based analysis within Power BI!

5.3. NOW and TODAY functions - Retrieving current time and date

In this section, we will explore the NOW and TODAY functions in DAX, which are invaluable tools for working with real-time data and capturing the current date and time in Power BI. These functions allow users to dynamically retrieve the system's current date and time, facilitating real-time analyses and time-sensitive calculations.

5.3.1 Understanding Real-Time Data Analysis

Real-time data analysis is becoming increasingly important for businesses as they strive to make timely and data-driven decisions. Whether it's monitoring key performance indicators (KPIs), tracking social media trends, or managing stock market data, having access to the current date and time is critical for making accurate and up-to-date analyses.

The NOW and TODAY functions in DAX provide an efficient way to capture the current date and time within Power BI reports, making real-time data analysis more accessible and effective.

5.3.2 The NOW Function

The NOW function in DAX is used to retrieve the current date and time from the system's clock. It does not require any arguments and returns the current date and time as a DateTime value.

The syntax of the NOW function is as follows:

```
NOW()
```

For example, let's consider a Sales table in which we want to capture the exact date and time of each transaction. We can create a calculated column using the NOW function as follows:

```
Transaction DateTime = NOW()
```

The "Transaction DateTime" column will display the current date and time for each transaction in the Sales table.

5.3.3 The TODAY Function

The TODAY function in DAX is similar to the NOW function, but it retrieves only the current date without the time component. Like the NOW function, the TODAY function does not require any arguments and returns the current date as a Date value.

The syntax of the TODAY function is as follows:

```

```

TODAY()
```

For instance, suppose we have a Project table in which we want to record the date on which each project was initiated. We can create a calculated column using the TODAY function as follows:

```

Project Start Date = TODAY()
```

The "Project Start Date" column will display the current date for each project's start date.

### 5.3.4 Use Cases for NOW and TODAY Functions

The NOW and TODAY functions are versatile and can be applied to various use cases that require real-time data analysis or time-sensitive calculations.

1. Tracking Time of Data Entry: When capturing data in real-time, such as when recording customer inquiries or service requests, using the NOW function can be valuable for tracking the exact time when the data was entered.

2. Monitoring KPIs: In a business dashboard, using the TODAY function can assist in tracking KPIs for the current day, providing a real-time view of key metrics.
```

3. Timestamping Records: For data audit purposes, using the NOW function can help add a timestamp to records when certain events occur, such as when orders are placed or inventory is updated.

4. Real-Time Stock Market Analysis: In financial analysis, using the NOW function is crucial for real-time monitoring of stock market data, enabling traders and investors to make timely decisions.

5. Time-Dependent Calculations: The NOW and TODAY functions can be combined with other DAX expressions to perform time-dependent calculations, such as identifying overdue tasks or measuring response times.

5.3.5 Handling Real-Time Data Refresh

When working with real-time data analysis in Power BI, it is essential to consider the data refresh settings. By default, Power BI automatically refreshes data at regular intervals. However, for real-time scenarios, users may need to adjust the data refresh frequency to ensure that the data remains up to date.

Users should also be mindful of the performance impact of real-time data refresh, as more frequent data updates may lead to increased resource consumption. Careful planning and optimization of data refresh settings are necessary to strike a balance between real-time data analysis and system performance.

5.3.6 Combining NOW and TODAY Functions with Time Intelligence

The NOW and TODAY functions can be used in combination with other time intelligence functions and DAX expressions to perform more sophisticated time-based calculations. For instance, consider a Sales table with a "Transaction Date" column. We can create a measure to calculate the total sales for the current month using the NOW and MONTH functions:

```
Current Month Sales =
CALCULATE(
    SUM(Sales[Revenue]),
    FILTER(
        Sales,
        MONTH(Sales[Transaction Date]) = MONTH(NOW())
    )
)
```

In this example, the "Current Month Sales" measure will calculate the total revenue for the current month by filtering the sales data based on the month of the "Transaction Date" column and comparing it to the month of the current date retrieved using the NOW function.

5.3.7 Using Functions in Calculated Columns and Measures

Both the NOW and TODAY functions, along with other time intelligence functions, can be used in calculated columns, measures, and calculated tables. Their ability to dynamically capture the current date and time makes them powerful assets for real-time data analysis and time-sensitive calculations.

5.3.8 Additional Considerations

When using the NOW and TODAY functions, it is crucial to be mindful of the time zone settings in Power BI, especially when working with data from different regions or time zones. Inaccurate time zone configurations may lead to discrepancies in real-time data analyses.

Furthermore, users should be aware of any potential data inconsistencies or missing values in date and time columns, as they may impact the accuracy of real-time calculations.

In conclusion, the NOW and TODAY functions in DAX play a vital role in real-time data analysis and time-sensitive calculations within Power BI. By capturing the current date and time, users can perform various real-time analyses and make data-driven decisions based on the most up-to-date information. When combined with other time intelligence functions and DAX expressions, the NOW and TODAY functions become powerful tools for conducting sophisticated time-based analyses. As we continue our exploration of DAX in subsequent chapters, we will discover more advanced date and time functions and techniques to further enhance our time-based analytics and leverage the full capabilities of real-time data analysis within Power BI!

CHAPTER VI
Calculating Financial Data with DAX

6.1. NPV and IRR functions - Calculating Net Present Value and Internal Rate of Return

In this chapter, we will explore the NPV (Net Present Value) and IRR (Internal Rate of Return) functions in DAX, which are essential for financial data analysis in Power BI. These functions enable users to evaluate the profitability of investments, projects, and financial decisions by calculating the Net Present Value and Internal Rate of Return.

6.1.1 Understanding Financial Data Analysis

Financial data analysis is a critical aspect of decision-making for individuals and businesses alike. It involves analyzing financial data to assess the performance, profitability, and viability of investments, projects, and business strategies. Two fundamental financial metrics used in such analysis are the Net Present Value (NPV) and Internal Rate of Return (IRR).

The NPV represents the difference between the present value of cash inflows and outflows associated with an investment or project. A positive NPV indicates that the investment is profitable, while a negative NPV suggests that the investment may not be economically viable.

On the other hand, the IRR is the discount rate at which the NPV of cash flows becomes zero, signifying the rate of return at which the investment breaks even. The IRR is a vital metric for comparing different investment opportunities and assessing their potential returns.

6.1.2 The NPV Function

The NPV function in DAX is used to calculate the Net Present Value of a series of cash flows based on a specified discount rate. It takes two arguments: the discount rate and a table containing cash flow values.

The syntax of the NPV function is as follows:

```
NPV(<discount_rate>, <cash_flows_table>)
```

Here, `<discount_rate>` represents the rate of return used to discount future cash flows to their present value, and `<cash_flows_table>` is a table containing cash flow values.

For example, let's consider an investment project with projected cash flows for five years stored in a table named "Cash Flows." To calculate the Net Present Value of the investment using a discount rate of 10%, we can use the NPV function as follows:

```
Net Present Value = NPV(0.10, 'Cash Flows')
```

The "Net Present Value" measure will display the NPV of the cash flows based on the specified discount rate.

6.1.3 The IRR Function

The IRR function in DAX is used to calculate the Internal Rate of Return of a series of cash flows. It takes one argument, which is a table containing cash flow values.

The syntax of the IRR function is as follows:

```
IRR(<cash_flows_table>)
```

Here, `<cash_flows_table>` is a table containing cash flow values.

For instance, let's use the same "Cash Flows" table from the previous example to calculate the Internal Rate of Return of the investment:

```
Internal Rate of Return = IRR('Cash Flows')
```

The "Internal Rate of Return" measure will display the IRR of the cash flows.

6.1.4 Handling Irregular Cash Flows

It's important to note that the NPV and IRR functions assume a consistent pattern of cash flows with equal time intervals. In real-world scenarios, cash flows may be irregular, occurring at different time points. To use the NPV and IRR functions effectively, users may need to adjust or interpolate cash flows to ensure a consistent time interval between them.

Additionally, cash flows must include both initial investments (negative values) and subsequent returns (positive values) for accurate NPV and IRR calculations.

6.1.5 Using NPV and IRR for Decision-Making

The NPV and IRR functions are powerful tools for evaluating investment opportunities and making informed financial decisions. When comparing multiple projects or investment options, users can use these functions to assess which option yields the highest NPV or offers the most attractive IRR.

For instance, suppose a company is considering two projects with projected cash flows for the next five years. By calculating the NPV and IRR for each project, the company can identify the more profitable investment and make decisions based on the financial metrics.

6.1.6 Handling Discount Rates

The discount rate used in NPV calculations plays a crucial role in determining the present value of future cash flows. Different projects may warrant different discount rates based on factors such as risk, inflation, and market conditions.

Users should carefully select an appropriate discount rate that accurately reflects the opportunity cost of capital for the specific investment or project under consideration.

6.1.7 Sensitivity Analysis with NPV and IRR

The NPV and IRR functions can also be used in sensitivity analysis, which involves assessing the impact of changes in inputs, such as discount rates or cash flow projections, on the financial metrics.

By running various scenarios with different discount rates or cash flow assumptions, decision-makers can gain insights into the sensitivity of the project's profitability to different factors. This helps in identifying potential risks and making more informed investment decisions.

6.1.8 Using Functions in Measures and Calculated Columns

Both the NPV and IRR functions, along with other DAX expressions, can be used to create calculated columns or measures in Power BI. This allows users to visualize and analyze financial metrics dynamically in reports and dashboards.

6.1.9 Additional Considerations

When using the NPV and IRR functions, it is essential to validate the accuracy of cash flow projections and discount rates. Errors or incorrect data inputs can lead to unreliable results and misinformed decisions.

Furthermore, users should be cautious of using these functions with a large number of cash flow values over extended periods, as the calculations may be resource-intensive and impact report performance.

In conclusion, the NPV and IRR functions in DAX are crucial tools for financial data analysis in Power BI. They allow users to calculate the Net Present Value and Internal Rate of Return of investments and projects, aiding in decision-making and performance evaluation. By using these functions alongside other DAX expressions, users can gain deeper insights into the profitability and financial viability of different opportunities. As we continue our exploration of DAX in subsequent chapters, we will discover more advanced financial functions and techniques to further enhance our financial data analysis capabilities within Power BI!

6.2. PV and FV functions - Calculating Present Value and Future Value of cash flows

In this section, we will delve into the PV (Present Value) and FV (Future Value) functions in DAX, essential tools for financial data analysis in Power BI. These functions allow users to calculate the present value and future value of cash flows, enabling them to evaluate the worth of investments, loans, and financial decisions over time.

6.2.1 Understanding Present Value and Future Value

The concepts of Present Value (PV) and Future Value (FV) are fundamental in finance, serving as critical indicators for decision-making and financial planning. Both PV and FV involve the evaluation of cash flows over time, taking into account the impact of interest rates and time periods.

Present Value (PV) refers to the current value of a future sum of money, discounted at a specific rate of return (interest rate). In other words, it represents the worth of a future cash flow in terms of its value today. PV calculations help individuals and businesses assess the attractiveness of investments or projects, considering the time value of money.

Future Value (FV), on the other hand, represents the value of an investment or cash flow at a specific point in the future, taking into account the compounding effect of interest over time. FV calculations are crucial for financial planning, enabling individuals and businesses to project the growth of investments or savings over a given period.

6.2.2 The PV Function

The PV function in DAX is used to calculate the Present Value of a future cash flow, discounted at a specified interest rate and period. It takes three arguments: the interest rate, the number of periods, and the future cash flow.

The syntax of the PV function is as follows:

```
PV(<interest_rate>, <number_of_periods>, <future_cash_flow>)
```

Here, `<interest_rate>` represents the discount rate or interest rate used to discount the future cash flow, `<number_of_periods>` is the number of periods over which the cash flow is discounted, and `<future_cash_flow>` is the future cash flow amount.

For example, suppose we are considering an investment with a projected cash flow of $10,000 after three years, and the discount rate is 5%. To calculate the Present Value of the cash flow, we can use the PV function as follows:

```
Present Value = PV(0.05, 3, 10000)
```

The "Present Value" measure will display the worth of the future cash flow in terms of its current value based on the specified interest rate and time period.

6.2.3 The FV Function

The FV function in DAX is used to calculate the Future Value of an investment or cash flow after a specific number of periods, considering compounding interest. It takes three arguments: the interest rate, the number of periods, and the present cash flow.

The syntax of the FV function is as follows:

```
FV(<interest_rate>, <number_of_periods>, <present_cash_flow>)
```

Here, `<interest_rate>` represents the rate of return or interest rate applied to the cash flow, `<number_of_periods>` is the number of periods over which the cash flow is compounded, and `<present_cash_flow>` is the initial cash flow amount.

For instance, let's assume we have an investment of $5,000 with an annual interest rate of 8%, and we want to calculate the Future Value of the investment after five years. We can use the FV function as follows:

```
Future Value = FV(0.08, 5, -5000)
```

The "Future Value" measure will display the worth of the investment after five years, considering the compounded interest.

6.2.4 Handling Different Cash Flow Frequencies

The PV and FV functions assume a consistent frequency of cash flows over regular periods. However, in real-world scenarios, cash flows may not occur at fixed intervals. For irregular cash flow patterns, users may need to interpolate or adjust the cash flows to align them with the time periods used in the PV and FV calculations.

Moreover, users should consider the time period used in the interest rate when discounting or compounding cash flows. The interest rate should be consistent with the cash flow frequency to ensure accurate PV and FV calculations.

6.2.5 Using PV and FV for Decision-Making

The PV and FV functions are valuable tools for making informed financial decisions. When evaluating investment opportunities or loans, users can use these functions to compare the present value of cash inflows and outflows or determine the future value of an investment over time.

For instance, suppose a company is considering two investment projects with different cash flow patterns. By calculating the PV and FV for each project, the company can identify the most financially rewarding option or evaluate the long-term impact of investment decisions.

6.2.6 Sensitivity Analysis with PV and FV

Similar to NPV and IRR, the PV and FV functions can also be used in sensitivity analysis. By varying the interest rate or the number of periods, decision-makers can assess the impact of changes in assumptions on the present and future values of cash flows.

Sensitivity analysis helps users understand the potential risks and uncertainties associated with financial decisions, enabling them to make more robust and well-informed choices.

6.2.7 Using Functions in Measures and Calculated Columns

Both the PV and FV functions, along with other DAX expressions, can be used to create calculated columns or measures in Power BI. This allows users to visualize and analyze the present and future values of investments dynamically in reports and dashboards.

6.2.8 Additional Considerations

When using the PV and FV functions, users should ensure that the interest rate used aligns with the frequency of cash flows and the time periods involved. Mismatched assumptions may lead to inaccurate results and misinterpretations.

Additionally, it is essential to verify the accuracy of cash flow projections and interest rate inputs, as errors or incorrect data can significantly impact the validity of PV and FV calculations.

In conclusion, the PV and FV functions in DAX are powerful tools for financial data analysis in Power BI. They enable users to evaluate the present and future values of investments, loans, and financial decisions, supporting informed decision-making and financial planning. By using these functions alongside other DAX expressions, users can gain deeper insights into the worth and potential returns of different financial opportunities. As we continue our exploration of DAX in subsequent chapters, we will discover more advanced financial functions and techniques to further enhance our financial data analysis capabilities within Power BI!

6.3. RATE and NPER functions - Calculating interest rates and number of periods

In this section, we will explore the RATE and NPER functions in DAX, crucial tools for financial data analysis in Power BI. These functions facilitate the calculation of interest rates and the number of periods required to achieve specific financial goals, making them essential for loan calculations, investment planning, and financial decision-making.

6.3.1 Understanding Interest Rates and Number of Periods

Interest rates and the number of periods are key components in financial calculations, determining the cost of borrowing or the potential returns on investments over time. Whether it's securing a loan or planning for retirement, understanding the interest rate or the time required to reach a financial objective is critical for making informed decisions.

The RATE function calculates the interest rate per period needed to reach a specific financial goal, given a series of equal periodic payments and a predetermined final value. On the other hand, the NPER function calculates the number of periods required to achieve a financial goal, based on a fixed interest rate and a series of equal periodic payments.

6.3.2 The RATE Function

The RATE function in DAX is used to calculate the interest rate per period needed to reach a specified future value with a series of equal periodic payments (annuities). It takes three arguments: the number of periods, the payment amount, and the present value.

The syntax of the RATE function is as follows:

```
RATE(<number_of_periods>, <payment_amount>, <present_value>)
```

Here, `<number_of_periods>` represents the total number of payment periods, `<payment_amount>` is the amount paid each period, and `<present_value>` is the present value of the annuity.

For example, let's consider an investment with a present value of $10,000, regular monthly payments of $500, and a duration of 36 months. To calculate the interest rate required to achieve the future value, we can use the RATE function as follows:

```
Interest Rate per Period = RATE(36, -500, 10000)
```

The "Interest Rate per Period" measure will display the interest rate needed to reach the future value of the annuity.

6.3.3 The NPER Function

The NPER function in DAX is used to calculate the number of periods required to reach a specific financial goal with a series of equal periodic payments (annuities). It takes three arguments: the interest rate per period, the payment amount, and the future value.

The syntax of the NPER function is as follows:

```
NPER(<interest_rate_per_period>, <payment_amount>, <future_value>)
```

Here, `<interest_rate_per_period>` represents the interest rate per period, `<payment_amount>` is the amount paid each period, and `<future_value>` is the desired future value of the annuity.

For instance, suppose an individual wants to save $20,000 for a down payment on a house by saving $500 per month. If the annual interest rate is 6%, we can calculate the number of months required to reach the financial goal using the NPER function:

```
Number of Periods = NPER(0.06/12, -500, 20000)
```

The "Number of Periods" measure will display the number of months required to accumulate $20,000 with the given monthly savings and interest rate.

6.3.4 Handling Different Payment Frequencies

Both the RATE and NPER functions assume equal periodic payments at consistent intervals. In practice, financial transactions may involve varying payment frequencies, such as monthly, quarterly, or annually. To use these functions effectively, users may need to adjust the payment frequency and interest rate accordingly.

Users should ensure that the payment frequency and interest rate align with each other to yield accurate results in RATE and NPER calculations.

6.3.5 Using RATE and NPER for Loan Calculations

The RATE and NPER functions are particularly useful for loan calculations, helping users determine the interest rate or the number of periods required to repay a loan within a specific time frame.

For example, a borrower can use the RATE function to calculate the interest rate on a loan based on the fixed monthly payments and the loan amount. Alternatively, a lender can use the NPER function to calculate the number of monthly payments required for a borrower to repay the loan fully.

6.3.6 Planning for Investments and Savings

In addition to loan calculations, the RATE and NPER functions are valuable for investment planning and savings goals. Investors can use these functions to determine the interest rate required to achieve a specific investment target or the number of periods needed to reach their financial objectives.

For instance, an individual saving for retirement can use the NPER function to determine how many years of contributions are needed to accumulate a desired retirement fund based on a fixed annual interest rate.

6.3.7 Sensitivity Analysis with RATE and NPER

Similar to other financial functions, RATE and NPER can be used in sensitivity analysis. Decision-makers can explore different interest rate scenarios or durations to understand how changes in assumptions impact loan repayments or savings goals.

Sensitivity analysis provides valuable insights into the risks and uncertainties associated with financial planning, helping users make more informed and robust decisions.

6.3.8 Using Functions in Measures and Calculated Columns

Both the RATE and NPER functions, along with other DAX expressions, can be used to create calculated columns or measures in Power BI. This allows users to visualize and analyze interest rates and the number of periods dynamically in reports and dashboards.

6.3.9 Additional Considerations

When using the RATE and NPER functions, it is crucial to verify the accuracy of payment amounts, present values, future values, and interest rate inputs. Errors or incorrect data can significantly impact the validity of the calculated results.

Additionally, users should be mindful of using these functions in scenarios with varying interest rates or irregular cash flows, as they may require more advanced financial modeling techniques.

In conclusion, the RATE and NPER functions in DAX are essential tools for financial data analysis in Power BI. They enable users to calculate interest rates and the number of periods required to achieve specific financial goals, supporting loan calculations, investment planning, and decision-making. By using these functions alongside other DAX expressions, users can gain deeper insights into loan repayment schedules, savings targets, and the impact of interest rates on financial decisions. As we continue our exploration of DAX in subsequent chapters, we will discover more advanced financial functions and techniques to further enhance our financial data analysis capabilities within Power BI!

CHAPTER VII
Logic and Relationship Functions in DAX

7.1 AND, OR, and NOT Functions - Handling Logical Expressions

In this chapter, we will explore the logic and relationship functions in DAX, focusing on the AND, OR, and NOT functions. These functions play a crucial role in filtering and evaluating data based on logical conditions, allowing users to perform complex data analysis and make informed decisions.

7.1.1 Understanding Logical Expressions

Logical expressions are statements that evaluate to either TRUE or FALSE based on certain conditions. These conditions can involve comparisons, calculations, or a combination of multiple conditions. Logic functions in DAX enable users to evaluate these expressions and manipulate data accordingly.

The AND, OR, and NOT functions are fundamental in logical expressions. They allow users to combine multiple conditions, create compound expressions, and negate existing conditions.

7.1.2 The AND Function

The AND function in DAX is used to combine multiple logical expressions and return TRUE only if all conditions are TRUE. If any of the conditions are FALSE, the AND function returns FALSE.

The syntax of the AND function is as follows:

```
AND(<condition1>, <condition2>, ..., <conditionN>)
```

Here, `<condition1>`, `<condition2>`, ..., and `<conditionN>` are the logical expressions that the function evaluates.

For example, consider a dataset of sales transactions where we want to filter for orders that were both made in the United States (Country = "USA") and have a sales amount greater than $1,000. We can use the AND function as follows:

```
Filtered Sales = FILTER('Sales', AND('Sales'[Country] = "USA", 'Sales'[Amount] > 1000))
```

The "Filtered Sales" table will contain only the sales records that satisfy both conditions: being from the USA and having an amount greater than $1,000.

7.1.3 The OR Function

The OR function in DAX is used to evaluate multiple logical expressions and return TRUE if at least one of the conditions is TRUE. It returns FALSE only when all conditions are FALSE.

The syntax of the OR function is as follows:

```
OR(<condition1>, <condition2>, ..., <conditionN>)
```

Similar to the AND function, `<condition1>`, `<condition2>`, ..., and `<conditionN>` are the logical expressions that the function evaluates.

For instance, consider a scenario where we want to filter for orders with either a sales amount greater than $2,000 or from customers in the "Premium" category. We can use the OR function as follows:

```
High-Value Orders = FILTER('Orders', OR('Orders'[Amount] > 2000, 'Orders'[Category] = "Premium"))
```

The "High-Value Orders" table will contain sales records that meet either of the conditions: having a sales amount exceeding $2,000 or being from customers in the "Premium" category.

7.1.4 The NOT Function

The NOT function in DAX is used to reverse the result of a logical expression. If the original expression evaluates to TRUE, the NOT function returns FALSE, and vice versa.

The syntax of the NOT function is as follows:

```
NOT(<condition>)
```

Here, `<condition>` is the logical expression that the function negates.

For example, consider a dataset of product inventory where we want to filter for products that are not currently out of stock. We can use the NOT function as follows:

```
Available Products = FILTER('Products', NOT('Products'[StockStatus] = "Out of Stock"))
```

The "Available Products" table will contain product records that are not marked as "Out of Stock."

7.1.5 Combining Logic Functions

Logic functions can be combined to create more complex logical expressions using parentheses to define the order of evaluation. This allows users to perform advanced filtering and calculations based on multiple conditions.

For instance, consider a scenario where we want to filter for orders that are from the USA, have a sales amount greater than $1,000, and are not in the "Pending" status. We can use a combination of AND and NOT functions as follows:

```
Filtered Sales = FILTER('Sales', AND('Sales'[Country] = "USA", 'Sales'[Amount] > 1000,
NOT('Sales'[Status] = "Pending")))
```

The "Filtered Sales" table will contain sales records that meet all three conditions: being from the USA, having a sales amount greater than $1,000, and not being in the "Pending" status.

7.1.6 Using Logic Functions for Calculations

Logic functions are not limited to filtering data but can also be used in calculated columns or measures. This allows users to create dynamic calculations based on logical conditions.

For example, suppose we want to categorize sales transactions as "High" or "Low" based on whether the sales amount is greater than $2,000 or not. We can use the IF function in combination with the OR function as follows:

```
Sales Category = IF(OR('Sales'[Amount] > 2000), "High", "Low")
```

The "Sales Category" column will display "High" for sales transactions with amounts greater than $2,000 and "Low" for others.

7.1.7 Enhancing Data Analysis with Logic Functions

Logic functions are powerful tools that enhance data analysis in Power BI. By combining logical expressions, users can create dynamic filters, perform advanced calculations, and gain deeper insights into their data.

These functions allow for more sophisticated business intelligence scenarios, such as customer segmentation, trend analysis, and anomaly detection, enabling users to make data-driven decisions with greater accuracy and confidence.

7.1.8 Additional Considerations

When using logic functions, users should ensure that the logical expressions are properly constructed and that the parentheses are placed correctly to avoid unintended results. Logical errors can lead to inaccurate data analysis and conclusions.

Moreover, users should be mindful of the data type of the fields involved in logical expressions, as incorrect data types may lead to unexpected outcomes.

In conclusion, the AND, OR, and NOT functions in DAX are essential components for handling logical expressions and relationship evaluation in Power BI. They allow users to filter data, perform complex calculations, and make data-driven decisions based on specific conditions. By leveraging these logic functions alongside other DAX expressions, users can gain a deeper understanding of their data and uncover valuable insights for better business intelligence and analytics. As we proceed with our exploration of DAX in the following chapters, we will discover more advanced logic and relationship functions to further expand our data analysis capabilities within Power BI!

7.2 RELATED Function - Linking Data Tables

In this chapter, we will delve into the RELATED function in DAX, a powerful tool that facilitates the establishment of relationships between data tables in Power BI. The RELATED function plays a critical role in data analysis, enabling users to access information from related tables and perform cross-table calculations to gain deeper insights into their data.

7.2.1 Understanding Data Relationships

In relational databases and data models, data is often organized into multiple tables connected by common fields, forming relationships between the tables. These relationships help to avoid data duplication and ensure data integrity by maintaining data consistency across the tables.

In Power BI, data relationships allow users to create meaningful connections between different data tables based on shared columns, known as foreign keys and primary keys. By establishing relationships, users can navigate through related tables to retrieve relevant information and perform calculations involving data from multiple tables.

7.2.2 The RELATED Function

The RELATED function in DAX is used to access data from a related table based on the existing data relationships. It allows users to retrieve information from a related table using a common field (foreign key) as a reference. The function automatically follows the data relationship to return the related data.

The syntax of the RELATED function is as follows:

```
RELATED(<column_name>)
```

Here, `<column_name>` is the name of the column in the related table that contains the data to be retrieved.

For example, consider a data model with two tables: "Sales" and "Products." The "Sales" table contains sales transaction data, including the product ID for each sale. The "Products" table contains detailed information about each product, including the product name and price. A data relationship is established between the "Sales" table and the "Products" table based on the common "Product ID" column.

Now, if we want to display the product name for each sale in the "Sales" table, we can use the RELATED function as follows:

```
Sales with Product Names = ADDCOLUMNS('Sales', "Product Name",
RELATED('Products'[Product Name]))
```

The "Sales with Product Names" table will contain the sales data along with the corresponding product names retrieved from the "Products" table based on the established relationship.

7.2.3 Utilizing RELATED in Calculations

The RELATED function is not limited to data retrieval; it can also be used in calculated columns and measures to perform cross-table calculations and analysis. By combining the RELATED function with other DAX functions, users can create powerful calculations that involve data from multiple related tables.

For instance, suppose we want to calculate the total revenue for each sale by multiplying the sales quantity with the product price. We can use the RELATED function along with other DAX functions as follows:

```
```

Total Revenue = SUMX('Sales', RELATED('Products'[Product Price]) * 'Sales'[Quantity])
```
```

The "Total Revenue" measure will calculate the total revenue for each sale based on the sales quantity and the product price retrieved from the "Products" table.

7.2.4 Handling Relationships and Filter Context

When using the RELATED function, it is crucial to understand the concept of filter context in Power BI. The filter context refers to the current set of filters applied to the data, such as slicers, visuals, or filter conditions in DAX calculations.

The RELATED function respects the filter context, meaning that the function considers the active filters to retrieve the related data. This ensures that the function returns accurate and contextually relevant information.

However, users should be mindful of the potential impact of the filter context on calculations involving RELATED. Incorrect or unintended filters can lead to unexpected results or incomplete data retrieval.

7.2.5 Managing Many-to-One and One-to-Many Relationships

In data modeling, relationships can be classified as either many-to-one or one-to-many. Many-to-one relationships indicate that multiple records in one table can be related to a single record in another table. On the other hand, one-to-many relationships indicate that a single record in one table can be related to multiple records in another table.

The direction of the relationship is essential when using the RELATED function. For many-to-one relationships, the RELATED function works seamlessly, as it always follows the direction of the relationship. However, for one-to-many relationships, users may need to employ other functions, such as RELATEDTABLE or SUMMARIZE, to retrieve data in the desired direction.

7.2.6 Understanding Filter Propagation

Filter propagation is another crucial aspect of data relationships in Power BI. When filtering data in one table, the filter can propagate through the relationships to affect data in related tables. This behavior ensures that data remains consistent and accurate across the entire data model.

The RELATED function respects the filter propagation, meaning that the function considers the propagated filters when retrieving related data. As a result, the function returns information that aligns with the applied filters.

7.2.7 Addressing Circular Relationships

Circular relationships occur when two or more tables have relationships that form a loop, potentially leading to ambiguous results. Power BI automatically detects and handles circular relationships by allowing users to specify the direction of the relationship. This ensures that the RELATED function follows the desired path and avoids confusion.

7.2.8 Optimizing Performance with RELATED

To ensure optimal performance, users should be mindful of the data model's size and complexity when utilizing the RELATED function. While the function is a powerful tool for data analysis, excessive usage in large data models may impact query performance.

To enhance performance, users can consider creating calculated columns or measures that incorporate RELATED selectively, focusing on the most critical analysis scenarios.

7.2.9 Enhancing Data Analysis with RELATED

The RELATED function is a vital component in creating meaningful data relationships and conducting comprehensive data analysis in Power BI. By utilizing RELATED, users can effortlessly access data from related tables, perform cross-table calculations, and gain deeper insights into their data.

With the ability to navigate through relationships, retrieve contextually relevant information, and create dynamic calculations, users can leverage the full potential of data relationships in Power BI.

7.2.10 Additional Considerations

When using the RELATED function, users should ensure the accuracy and consistency of the data relationships. Properly defined relationships based on appropriate primary and foreign keys are crucial for the function's effectiveness.

Additionally, users should be aware of potential circular relationships, filter propagation, and filter context to avoid unintended results in their data analysis.

In conclusion, the RELATED function in DAX is a fundamental tool for linking data tables and enabling cross-table analysis in Power BI. By establishing relationships and leveraging the

RELATED function, users can access related data, perform complex calculations, and gain valuable insights into their data. As we continue our exploration of DAX in subsequent chapters, we will discover more logic and relationship functions to further expand our data analysis capabilities within Power BI!

7.3 CALCULATE and FILTER Functions - Customizing Calculations and Data Filtering

In this chapter, we will explore the CALCULATE and FILTER functions in DAX, powerful tools that allow users to customize calculations and data filtering in Power BI. These functions play a crucial role in modifying the context of calculations and applying specific filters to data, enabling users to perform more advanced analysis and gain deeper insights into their data.

7.3.1 Understanding Context in DAX

In DAX, context refers to the set of filters or conditions applied to the data when performing calculations. Context is essential for interpreting the data in a meaningful way, as it influences the results of calculations and aggregations.

Power BI automatically creates context based on the user's interactions with the report, such as selecting data points on visuals, applying slicers, or using filters. However, there are scenarios where users may need to customize the context to achieve specific analysis goals. This is where the CALCULATE and FILTER functions come into play.

7.3.2 The CALCULATE Function

The CALCULATE function in DAX is used to modify the filter context of a calculation or aggregation. It allows users to apply additional filters or remove existing filters for a particular calculation, ensuring that the desired context is considered.

The syntax of the CALCULATE function is as follows:

```
```
```

```
CALCULATE(<expression>, <filter1>, <filter2>, ...)
```
```
```

Here, `<expression>` represents the calculation or measure to be modified, and `<filter1>`, `<filter2>`, and so on, represent the filters that the function applies.

For example, suppose we have a measure called "Total Sales" that calculates the sum of sales amounts. If we want to calculate the total sales amount only for a specific region, such as "North," we can use the CALCULATE function as follows:

```
```
```

```
Total Sales (North) = CALCULATE([Total Sales], 'Sales'[Region] = "North")
```
```
```

The "Total Sales (North)" measure will display the total sales amount for the "North" region, considering only the sales data filtered by the specified region.

7.3.3 Using Multiple Filters in CALCULATE

The CALCULATE function can accept multiple filters to further customize the context of the calculation. Users can combine different filters using logical operators (AND, OR) to achieve more complex analysis scenarios.

For example, let's say we want to calculate the total sales amount for the "North" region and for a specific product category, such as "Electronics." We can use the CALCULATE function with multiple filters as follows:

```
Total Sales (North, Electronics) = CALCULATE([Total Sales], 'Sales'[Region] = "North", 'Sales'[Category] = "Electronics")
```

The "Total Sales (North, Electronics)" measure will display the total sales amount for the "North" region and the "Electronics" product category, considering both filters simultaneously.

7.3.4 The FILTER Function

The FILTER function in DAX is used to create custom filters that target specific rows or columns within a table. It allows users to dynamically apply filters based on certain conditions or calculations, helping to extract relevant data for analysis.

The syntax of the FILTER function is as follows:

```
FILTER(<table>, <condition1>, <condition2>, ...)
```

Here, `<table>` represents the table to be filtered, and `<condition1>`, `<condition2>`, and so on, represent the conditions that the function applies.

For instance, suppose we want to filter the "Sales" table to include only sales transactions with amounts greater than $1,000. We can use the FILTER function as follows:

```
High-Value Sales = FILTER('Sales', 'Sales'[Amount] > 1000)
```

The "High-Value Sales" table will contain sales transactions with amounts greater than $1,000, filtered from the original "Sales" table.

7.3.5 Using FILTER with CALCULATE

The FILTER and CALCULATE functions can be used in conjunction to create even more powerful and dynamic calculations. By combining these functions, users can modify the context of calculations and filter data as needed for complex analysis scenarios.

For example, let's say we want to calculate the total sales amount for the "North" region and for a specific product category, "Electronics," while considering only sales transactions with amounts greater than $1,000. We can use both FILTER and CALCULATE functions as follows:

```
Total High-Value Sales (North, Electronics) =
CALCULATE([Total Sales],
    FILTER('Sales', 'Sales'[Region] = "North", 'Sales'[Category] = "Electronics", 'Sales'[Amount]
> 1000)
)
```

The "Total High-Value Sales (North, Electronics)" measure will display the total sales amount for the "North" region and the "Electronics" product category, considering only sales transactions with amounts greater than $1,000.

7.3.6 Handling Aggregations with CALCULATE

The CALCULATE function is particularly useful when dealing with aggregations in complex data models. By using CALCULATE, users can create more sophisticated aggregations that consider specific filters or data contexts.

For instance, suppose we want to calculate the average sales amount for each product category but only for sales transactions with amounts greater than $500. We can use the CALCULATE function with the AVERAGE function as follows:

```
Average Sales (High-Value) =

CALCULATE(AVERAGE('Sales'[Amount]), 'Sales'[Amount] > 500)
```

The "Average Sales (High-Value)" measure will display the average sales amount for each product category, considering only sales transactions with amounts greater than $500.

7.3.7 Using ALL and ALLEXCEPT with CALCULATE

The CALCULATE function can be further customized by using the ALL and ALLEXCEPT functions to control the filter context. The ALL function removes all filters from the specified column, while the ALLEXCEPT function retains the filter on the specified column and removes filters from other columns.

For example, suppose we want to calculate the total sales amount for each product category, ignoring any filters on the "Region" column. We can use the ALL function as follows:

```
Total Sales (Ignore Region) = CALCULATE([Total Sales], ALL('Sales'[Region]))
```

The "Total Sales (Ignore Region)" measure will display the total sales amount for each product category, regardless of any filters applied to the "Region" column.

7.3.8 Enhancing Data Analysis with CALCULATE and FILTER

The CALCULATE and FILTER functions are essential components for customizing calculations and data filtering in Power BI. By using these functions, users can dynamically modify the context of calculations, apply specific filters, and perform complex analysis based on various conditions.

These functions enable users to gain deeper insights into their data, conduct more advanced business intelligence, and make data-driven decisions with greater accuracy and precision.

7.3.9 Additional Considerations

When using the CALCULATE and FILTER functions, users should be mindful of the potential impact on query performance, especially when dealing with large data models. Overuse of these functions may affect the overall report responsiveness.

Moreover, users should verify the accuracy of the specified filters and ensure that the data context aligns with the intended analysis goals to obtain reliable and meaningful results.

In conclusion, the CALCULATE and FILTER functions in DAX are powerful tools for custom

izing calculations and data filtering in Power BI. By leveraging these functions, users can dynamically modify data context, create custom filters, and perform more advanced data analysis. As we proceed with our exploration of DAX in the following chapters, we will continue to uncover more functions and techniques to further expand our data analysis capabilities within Power BI!

CHAPTER VIII
Handling Errors and Blank Values in DAX

8.1 IFERROR and ISBLANK Functions - Dealing with Errors and Blank Values

In this chapter, we will explore the IFERROR and ISBLANK functions in DAX, essential tools for handling errors and blank values in Power BI. Dealing with errors and empty cells is a common challenge in data analysis, and these functions provide effective solutions to ensure accurate and reliable calculations.

8.1.1 Understanding Errors and Blank Values

Errors and blank values are common occurrences in data sets, especially when dealing with large and diverse data sources. Errors can arise from various reasons, such as division by zero, invalid calculations, or missing data. Blank values, on the other hand, represent cells or fields with no data recorded.

When performing calculations in Power BI, encountering errors or blank values can disrupt data analysis and lead to incorrect results. Therefore, it is essential to handle these scenarios appropriately to avoid misleading insights and ensure the accuracy of calculations.

8.1.2 The IFERROR Function

The IFERROR function in DAX is used to handle errors in calculations. It allows users to specify a default value or alternative calculation to be returned if an error occurs in the original expression.

The syntax of the IFERROR function is as follows:

```
IFERROR(<expression>, <value_if_error>)
```

Here, `<expression>` represents the calculation or measure to be evaluated, and `<value_if_error>` is the value to be returned if an error occurs during the evaluation of `<expression>`.

For example, let's say we have a measure called "Profit Margin," which calculates the profit margin for each product category. To avoid potential errors caused by dividing by zero when calculating profit margin, we can use the IFERROR function as follows:

```
Profit Margin (with Error Handling) = IFERROR([Total Profit] / [Total Revenue], 0)
```

The "Profit Margin (with Error Handling)" measure will calculate the profit margin for each product category. In case of any division by zero errors, it will return 0 as the default value.

8.1.3 The ISBLANK Function

The ISBLANK function in DAX is used to check for blank values in a column or expression. It returns TRUE if a cell or expression is blank and FALSE if it contains data.

The syntax of the ISBLANK function is as follows:

```
ISBLANK(<expression>)
```

Here, `<expression>` represents the column or cell to be checked for blank values.

For example, suppose we want to filter the "Sales" table to include only sales transactions with non-blank values in the "Customer Name" column. We can use the ISBLANK function in conjunction with the FILTER function as follows:

```
Sales with Customer Names = FILTER('Sales', NOT(ISBLANK('Sales'[Customer Name])))
```

The "Sales with Customer Names" table will contain sales transactions with non-blank values in the "Customer Name" column, excluding any records with blank customer names.

8.1.4 Using IFERROR and ISBLANK Together

The IFERROR and ISBLANK functions can be used in combination to handle both errors and blank values effectively. By incorporating these functions into calculations, users can ensure that calculations proceed smoothly, even in the presence of errors or missing data.

For instance, suppose we want to calculate the average sales amount for each product category but handle any blank values gracefully. We can use the IFERROR and ISBLANK functions as follows:

```
Average Sales (with Error Handling) =

IFERROR(AVERAGE('Sales'[Amount]), IF(ISBLANK(AVERAGE('Sales'[Amount])), 0))
```

The "Average Sales (with Error Handling)" measure will calculate the average sales amount for each product category. If there are any errors during the aggregation, it will return 0. Additionally, if the result of the average calculation is blank, it will also return 0.

8.1.5 Using BLANK Function

In addition to IFERROR and ISBLANK, the BLANK function in DAX can be utilized to explicitly return blank values. The BLANK function can be beneficial when defining default values or conditions in calculations.

The syntax of the BLANK function is as follows:

```
BLANK()
```

For example, suppose we want to calculate the average sales amount for each product category, but instead of returning 0 for blank results, we want to display the value as blank. We can use the BLANK function with IF as follows:

```
Average Sales (with Blank for Empty) =

IF(ISBLANK(AVERAGE('Sales'[Amount])), BLANK(), AVERAGE('Sales'[Amount]))
```

The "Average Sales (with Blank for Empty)" measure will calculate the average sales amount for each product category. If the result of the average calculation is blank, it will return a blank value instead of 0.

8.1.6 Handling Errors in Complex Calculations

Errors can occur in more complex calculations involving multiple expressions or nested functions. In such cases, it is essential to carefully consider each component of the calculation and apply error handling techniques accordingly.

For instance, let's say we have a measure that calculates the ratio of profit to revenue, and we want to handle any errors in the expression. We can use a combination of IFERROR functions within the calculation as follows:

```
Profit-to-Revenue Ratio (with Error Handling) =
IFERROR(
    DIVIDE([Total Profit], [Total Revenue]),
```

```
    IF(ISBLANK([Total Profit]), 0)

)
```
```

The "Profit-to-Revenue Ratio (with Error Handling)" measure will calculate the ratio of profit to revenue. If any errors occur during the calculation or if the profit value is blank, it will return 0.

### 8.1.7 Enhancing Data Analysis with Error Handling

Error handling with IFERROR and ISBLANK functions is crucial for ensuring data accuracy and avoiding disruptions in data analysis. By applying appropriate error handling techniques, users can create more robust and reliable calculations, providing accurate insights for decision-making.

These functions allow for smoother data visualization and reporting, as well as the ability to work with larger and more complex data sets without compromising data integrity.

### 8.1.8 Additional Considerations

When using IFERROR and ISBLANK functions, users should carefully consider the default values or alternative calculations provided. These values should align with the data context and analysis goals to ensure meaningful results.

Moreover, users should regularly validate data sources and perform data cleansing to minimize errors and blank values in their datasets. Data quality is essential for accurate data analysis and reliable calculations.
```

In conclusion, the IFERROR and ISBLANK functions in DAX are essential tools for handling errors and blank values in Power BI. By incorporating these functions into calculations, users can ensure the accuracy and reliability of their data analysis, providing valuable insights for decision-making processes. As we progress with our exploration of DAX in the following chapters, we will continue to discover more advanced techniques to enhance data analysis and expand our capabilities within Power BI!

8.2 COALESCE Function - Selecting the First Non-Empty Value

In this chapter, we will explore the COALESCE function in DAX, a valuable tool for handling blank values and errors by selecting the first non-empty value from a list of expressions. Dealing with blank values is crucial in data analysis to ensure accurate calculations and meaningful insights. The COALESCE function provides a concise and efficient way to manage such scenarios, enabling users to maintain data integrity and enhance the accuracy of their analysis.

8.2.1 Understanding Blank Values and Their Impact

Blank values, also known as null or missing values, can occur for various reasons in a dataset. They might be a result of incomplete data entry, missing information, or data gaps from different sources. When performing calculations or aggregations in Power BI, blank values can significantly impact the results, leading to incorrect or incomplete analysis.

Handling blank values is vital for producing reliable insights and making informed decisions based on accurate data. While blank values can be managed with IFERROR and ISBLANK functions, using the COALESCE function simplifies the process, especially when dealing with multiple expressions.

8.2.2 The COALESCE Function

The COALESCE function in DAX is used to evaluate a list of expressions and return the first non-empty value. If all the expressions in the list are blank, the COALESCE function will return a blank value.

The syntax of the COALESCE function is as follows:

```
COALESCE(<expression1>, <expression2>, ...)
```

Here, `<expression1>`, `<expression2>`, and so on, represent the list of expressions to be evaluated for non-empty values.

For example, suppose we have a measure called "Total Revenue" that calculates the total revenue for each product category. We also have an alternative measure called "Total Revenue (Alternate)" that calculates the total revenue using a different approach. To ensure that we always have a valid total revenue value, we can use the COALESCE function as follows:

```
Total Revenue (Final) = COALESCE([Total Revenue], [Total Revenue (Alternate)])
```

The "Total Revenue (Final)" measure will return the total revenue calculated by the "Total Revenue" measure if it is not blank. If "Total Revenue" is blank, it will return the total revenue calculated by the "Total Revenue (Alternate)" measure. This way, we always get a non-empty value for total revenue.

8.2.3 Using COALESCE with Multiple Expressions

The COALESCE function is particularly useful when dealing with multiple expressions that may contain blank values. It allows users to select the first non-empty value from a list of expressions, providing a streamlined approach to handle various scenarios.

For example, let's say we have three measures that calculate revenue for different regions: "Total Revenue (North)," "Total Revenue (South)," and "Total Revenue (West)." To get the total revenue for a specific region, we can use the COALESCE function as follows:

```
Total Revenue (Region) = COALESCE([Total Revenue (North)], [Total Revenue (South)], [Total Revenue (West)])
```

The "Total Revenue (Region)" measure will return the total revenue for the first non-blank value from the "Total Revenue (North)," "Total Revenue (South)," and "Total Revenue (West)" measures. This allows us to select the revenue value for a specific region efficiently.

8.2.4 Handling Errors with COALESCE

The COALESCE function is not limited to handling blank values; it can also manage errors in a similar manner. By including measures that handle errors in the list of expressions, users can ensure that the COALESCE function selects the first valid value available.

For example, let's say we have two measures: "Total Profit (with Error Handling)" and "Total Profit (Alternate)." If the "Total Profit (with Error Handling)" measure contains any errors, we can use the COALESCE function to select the valid value as follows:

```

```

Total Profit (Final) = COALESCE([Total Profit (with Error Handling)], [Total Profit (Alternate)])

```
```

The "Total Profit (Final)" measure will return the total profit calculated by the "Total Profit (with Error Handling)" measure if it is not blank or does not contain errors. If "Total Profit (with Error Handling)" contains errors, it will return the total profit calculated by the "Total Profit (Alternate)" measure, providing a reliable value for total profit.

8.2.5 Nested COALESCE Functions

The COALESCE function can be nested within other DAX functions to further enhance its capabilities. By combining COALESCE with other functions, users can create more complex expressions to handle various scenarios effectively.

For instance, let's say we have three measures: "Sales for North Region," "Sales for South Region," and "Sales for West Region." We want to calculate the total sales amount for the first non-blank and non-error value among these measures. We can use a nested COALESCE function as follows:

```
Total Sales (Region) =

COALESCE(

    [Sales for North Region],

    [Sales for South Region],

    [Sales for West Region]

)
```
```
```

The "Total Sales (Region)" measure will return the total sales amount for the first non-blank and non-error value among the "Sales for North Region," "Sales for South Region," and "Sales for West Region" measures.

8.2.6 Enhancing Data Analysis with COALESCE

The COALESCE function is a valuable tool for managing blank values and errors in Power BI. By selecting the first non-empty and valid value from a list of expressions, users can ensure accurate calculations and reliable data analysis.

Using COALESCE simplifies error handling and enhances the efficiency of data analysis, especially when dealing with complex data models or multiple expressions.

8.2.7 Additional Considerations

When using the COALESCE function, users should carefully arrange the expressions in the list to prioritize the desired order of evaluation. The first non-empty and non-error value encountered in the list will be

selected by COALESCE.

Moreover, users should regularly validate data sources and perform data cleansing to minimize blank values and errors in their datasets. Ensuring data quality is essential for accurate data analysis and reliable calculations.

In conclusion, the COALESCE function in DAX is a powerful tool for selecting the first non-empty and valid value from a list of expressions. By incorporating COALESCE into calculations, users can handle blank values and errors effectively, ensuring accurate data analysis and reliable insights. As we progress with our exploration of DAX in the following chapters, we will continue to discover more advanced techniques to enhance data analysis and expand our capabilities within Power BI!

CHAPTER IX
Combining DAX with Power Query and Power Pivot

9.1 Power Query - Extracting and Transforming Data

In this chapter, we will explore the integration of DAX with Power Query and Power Pivot, two essential components of Power BI that play a crucial role in data preparation and modeling. Power Query is a powerful data extraction and transformation tool that allows users to connect to various data sources, clean and reshape the data, and load it into Power BI for analysis. Power Pivot, on the other hand, is an in-memory data modeling engine that enables users to create sophisticated data models and perform advanced calculations using DAX.

9.1.1 Understanding Power Query and Its Capabilities

Power Query is a data transformation and mashup tool integrated into Power BI. It empowers users to connect to multiple data sources, including databases, Excel files, web services, and more, and retrieve the data they need for analysis. Power Query's intuitive user interface allows users to perform various data transformation tasks, such as filtering, sorting, merging, and aggregating, without the need for complex coding.

Key capabilities of Power Query include:

1. Data Connection: Power Query offers a wide range of data connectors, enabling users to connect to a vast array of data sources, both on-premises and in the cloud. Users can establish data connections with ease, making data retrieval seamless and efficient.

2. Data Transformation: With Power Query, users can clean and reshape data by applying various transformation steps. These steps include removing duplicates, splitting columns, replacing values, and pivoting data, among others.

3. Data Enrichment: Power Query allows users to enrich their data by merging it with other datasets or performing lookups to retrieve additional information from related tables.

4. Data Load: Once the data is transformed, users can load it into Power BI for further analysis using Power Pivot and DAX.

9.1.2 Using Power Query to Prepare Data for DAX Calculations

Data preparation is a crucial step in the data analysis process. Before performing calculations with DAX, data must be cleaned, transformed, and modeled appropriately. Power Query plays a vital role in this data preparation process, ensuring that the data is in the right format and structure for DAX calculations.

For example, suppose we have a dataset with sales data that includes product names, sales amounts, and dates. Before performing any DAX calculations, we may want to filter out irrelevant data, aggregate sales by product, and create relationships between tables. Power Query allows us to perform these tasks efficiently, providing a clean and organized dataset for DAX calculations.

9.1.3 Data Load and Data Model Creation

Once the data is prepared in Power Query, it can be loaded into Power Pivot to create a data model. Power Pivot is an in-memory data modeling engine that allows users to define relationships between tables, create calculated columns and measures using DAX, and build powerful data models for analysis.

The data model is the backbone of the Power BI report, as it determines how the data will be organized, aggregated, and visualized. With Power Pivot, users can create a flexible and efficient data model that supports complex calculations and interactive data exploration.

9.1.4 Integrating DAX with Power Pivot

DAX and Power Pivot work hand in hand to provide powerful data analysis capabilities in Power BI. DAX expressions can be used to create calculated columns and measures in the data model, allowing users to perform advanced calculations and define custom business logic.

For example, suppose we have a data model with sales data and want to create a calculated column that calculates the profit margin for each product. We can use DAX to define the calculation as follows:

```
Profit Margin = ( [Total Sales] - [Total Cost] ) / [Total Sales]
```

The "Profit Margin" calculated column will compute the profit margin for each product based on the "Total Sales" and "Total Cost" columns defined in the data model.

9.1.5 Leveraging DAX for Advanced Calculations

DAX provides a vast array of functions and features for performing complex calculations and aggregations. With DAX, users can create time intelligence calculations, perform ranking and filtering based on specific conditions, and implement various business logic scenarios.

For example, DAX offers functions like TOTALYTD, SAMEPERIODLASTYEAR, and RANKX, among others, that enable users to perform year-to-date calculations, compare data with the previous year, and rank items based on specific metrics.

9.1.6 Data Analysis and Visualization

With the data model created using Power Pivot and the advanced calculations performed using DAX, users can now analyze and visualize the data in Power BI. The data model serves as a foundation for creating interactive reports and dashboards that provide valuable insights and support data-driven decision-making.

Power BI's robust visualization capabilities enable users to present data in various chart types, such as bar charts, line charts, pie charts, and maps, among others. These visualizations can be further customized and interactively filtered to explore the data from different perspectives.

9.1.7 Benefits of Combining DAX with Power Query and Power Pivot

The integration of DAX with Power Query and Power Pivot brings numerous benefits to data analysis in Power BI:

- Data Integration: Power Query allows users to connect to multiple data sources and combine data from various origins into a single dataset for analysis using DAX.

- Data Transformation: Power Query enables users to clean and reshape data, ensuring it is in the right format and structure for DAX calculations.

- Data Modeling: Power Pivot provides a robust data modeling platform where users can create relationships, define hierarchies, and build sophisticated data models to support complex calculations.

- Advanced Calculations: DAX empowers users to perform advanced calculations, time intelligence functions, and custom aggregations, providing valuable insights for data analysis.

- Interactive Visualization: With the combination of DAX calculations and Power BI's visualization capabilities, users can create interactive and visually compelling reports and dashboards to present their findings effectively.

9.1.8 Conclusion

Combining DAX with Power Query and Power Pivot unlocks the full potential of Power BI as a comprehensive data analysis and visualization tool. Power Query's data extraction and transformation capabilities ensure that data is clean and organized for DAX calculations in Power Pivot. DAX, in turn, allows users to perform sophisticated calculations, enabling insightful data analysis and supporting data-driven decision-making.

By leveraging the synergy between DAX, Power Query, and Power Pivot, users can create dynamic and interactive reports that provide valuable insights, helping organizations gain a competitive edge through data-driven strategies. As we progress in our exploration of Power BI's capabilities, we will continue to uncover more advanced techniques and features to enhance data analysis and visualization.

9.2 Power Pivot - Building Data Models and Table Relationships

In this chapter, we will delve into Power Pivot, an integral part of Microsoft Power BI, and explore how it empowers users to build robust data models and establish table relationships. Power Pivot is a powerful in-memory data modeling engine that allows users to bring together and analyze vast amounts of data from various sources. By creating relationships between tables, users can effectively combine data, perform advanced calculations using DAX, and build comprehensive data models for insightful analysis and visualization.

9.2.1 Understanding Power Pivot and Its Role in Data Modeling

Power Pivot is a key component of Power BI that extends data analysis capabilities beyond traditional spreadsheet functionalities. With Power Pivot, users can work with larger datasets and perform complex data modeling tasks directly within the familiar Excel interface.

The main features and benefits of Power Pivot include:

1. In-Memory Data Model: Power Pivot operates in-memory, which means it stores data in RAM rather than reading from the original data source each time. This in-memory approach significantly speeds up data retrieval and calculations, enabling users to work with large datasets efficiently.

2. Multiple Data Sources: Power Pivot allows users to import data from various sources, including Excel workbooks, SQL databases, SharePoint lists, and other external data sources. This flexibility makes it easier to integrate data from different systems into a single data model.

3. Table Relationships: With Power Pivot, users can establish relationships between tables, creating a relational database-like structure within the data model. This relationship feature enables seamless data aggregation and analysis across multiple related tables.

4. Hierarchies and KPIs: Power Pivot supports the creation of hierarchies and Key Performance Indicators (KPIs), enhancing data organization and providing a better understanding of data trends and performance.

9.2.2 Creating a Data Model in Power Pivot

To start building a data model in Power Pivot, users need to first enable the Power Pivot add-in within Excel. Once enabled, they can access Power Pivot from the Excel ribbon and begin the process of importing data from various sources.

Users can load data from Excel tables, external databases, or other sources using Power Query to extract and transform the data. The Power Query Editor allows users to perform data cleaning, filtering, and shaping before loading it into Power Pivot.

After importing the data, users can define relationships between the different tables in the data model. Power Pivot's intuitive drag-and-drop interface makes establishing relationships simple, even for users without a background in database management.

9.2.3 Understanding Table Relationships

Table relationships are a fundamental aspect of data modeling in Power Pivot. By creating relationships between tables, users can combine data from multiple sources and perform consolidated analysis across related data.

In Power Pivot, relationships are based on one or more columns that serve as keys to link related tables. Commonly used relationship types include:

1. One-to-Many (1:N): In a one-to-many relationship, a value in one table can be linked to multiple values in another table. This relationship type is prevalent when analyzing transactional data, such as sales and customers.

2. Many-to-One (N:1): In a many-to-one relationship, multiple values in one table can be linked to a single value in another table. This relationship type is useful when analyzing data that involves categories and subcategories.

3. Many-to-Many (N:N): In a many-to-many relationship, multiple values in one table can be linked to multiple values in another table. This relationship type is typically implemented through a bridge table, which resolves the many-to-many relationship into two one-to-many relationships.

Understanding the nature of data and the relationships between tables is critical for building an effective data model that accurately represents the business scenario.

9.2.4 Creating Relationships in Power Pivot

To create relationships between tables in Power Pivot, users need to identify the columns that serve as keys for linking the tables. Once the appropriate columns are identified, users can drag and drop them into the diagram view, indicating the relationship type (one-to-many, many-to-one, or many-to-many).

Power Pivot automatically detects and suggests potential relationships based on column names and data types. However, users can modify and customize the relationships as needed to ensure accuracy and relevance in the data model.

9.2.5 Managing Relationships and Cardinality

Power Pivot allows users to manage relationships and define the cardinality between tables. Cardinality specifies how many unique values can exist on each side of the relationship.

For example, in a one-to-many relationship between the "Customers" table and the "Orders" table, the cardinality is 1:N. This means that each customer in the "Customers" table can be associated with multiple orders in the "Orders" table.

Understanding cardinality is crucial for correctly interpreting and analyzing data. By setting the cardinality, users ensure that data is aggregated and calculated appropriately across related tables.

9.2.6 Data Modeling with Power Pivot and DAX

Once the relationships between tables are established, users can utilize DAX expressions to perform advanced calculations and create calculated columns and measures in the data model.

DAX expressions can be used to calculate growth rates, perform year-over-year comparisons, and aggregate data based on various conditions. Additionally, DAX supports time intelligence functions, allowing users to perform dynamic time-based calculations, such as year-to-date and moving averages.

The integration of DAX with Power Pivot enhances the data model's analytical capabilities, providing users with insights and trends based on complex calculations and business logic.

9.2.7 Enhancing Data Analysis and Visualization

With a well-structured data model built in Power Pivot and advanced calculations performed using DAX, users can leverage the full potential of Power BI's data analysis and visualization features.

Power BI's interactive visualizations enable users to create dynamic reports and dashboards that respond to user interactions and filters. By using slicers, drill-downs, and cross-filtering, users can explore data from different perspectives and gain valuable insights into business performance and trends.

9.2.8 Benefits of Combining Power Query, Power

The combination of Power Query, Power Pivot, and DAX brings several benefits to data analysis in Power BI:

- Data Integration: Power Query allows users to connect to various data sources and combine data for analysis in Power Pivot.

- Data Transformation: Power Query enables users to clean and reshape data before loading it into Power Pivot, ensuring data accuracy and relevance.

- Data Modeling: Power Pivot facilitates the creation of a comprehensive data model with table relationships, hierarchies, and KPIs, providing a holistic view of the data.

- Advanced Calculations: DAX empowers users to perform sophisticated calculations and create custom measures and columns to support complex analysis.

- Interactive Visualization: Power BI's visualization capabilities allow users to create interactive and visually appealing reports and dashboards for data exploration and presentation.

9.2.9 Conclusion

Power Pivot is a powerful tool that complements Power Query and DAX, enabling users to build robust data models and establish table relationships for insightful data analysis in Power BI. By combining these components, users can transform raw data into meaningful insights, perform advanced calculations, and create interactive visualizations that support data-driven decision-making.

Understanding how to effectively use Power Query, Power Pivot, and DAX together is essential for maximizing the capabilities of Power BI and unlocking the full potential of data analysis and visualization. As we continue our exploration of Power BI's features, we will uncover more advanced techniques and strategies to enhance data modeling and analysis for a wide range of business scenarios.

9.3 Combining DAX, Power Query, and Power Pivot in Power BI

In this chapter, we will explore the seamless integration of DAX, Power Query, and Power Pivot in Power BI, and understand how these three components work together to deliver a powerful and comprehensive data analysis and visualization solution. By leveraging the strengths of each tool, users can transform raw data into meaningful insights, perform complex calculations, and create interactive reports and dashboards that support data-driven decision-making.

9.3.1 The Role of DAX, Power Query, and Power Pivot in Power BI

DAX, Power Query, and Power Pivot are three core components of Power BI, each serving a distinct purpose in the data analysis process:

1. Power Query: Power Query is the data extraction and transformation tool in Power BI. It allows users to connect to various data sources, clean and reshape data, and load it into Power BI for analysis. Power Query simplifies the data preparation process, ensuring that the data is in the right format and structure for analysis in Power Pivot.

2. Power Pivot: Power Pivot is the in-memory data modeling engine in Power BI. It allows users to create relationships between tables, define hierarchies, and build comprehensive data models. Power Pivot's in-memory approach enables fast data retrieval and calculations, even with large datasets.

3. DAX: Data Analysis Expressions (DAX) is the formula language used in Power BI to perform calculations and create custom measures and columns. DAX extends the analytical capabilities

of Power Pivot by enabling users to perform advanced calculations, time intelligence functions, and complex aggregations.

When combined, DAX, Power Query, and Power Pivot provide a complete solution for data analysis and visualization, allowing users to explore and understand data from multiple perspectives and gain valuable insights.

9.3.2 The Data Analysis Workflow in Power BI

The data analysis workflow in Power BI typically involves the following steps:

Step 1: Data Acquisition with Power Query

- Connect to Data Sources: Power Query allows users to connect to a wide range of data sources, including databases, files, web services, and cloud-based applications. Users can establish data connections and retrieve the required data for analysis.

- Data Transformation: With Power Query, users can perform data cleaning, filtering, and shaping to ensure the data is accurate and relevant. Data transformation steps include removing duplicates, splitting columns, changing data types, and handling missing values.

- Data Load: Once the data is transformed, it can be loaded into Power BI for further analysis using Power Pivot and DAX.

Step 2: Data Modeling with Power Pivot

- Create Data Model: Power Pivot enables users to create a data model by importing tables from Power Query and defining relationships between them. The data model serves as the foundation for all subsequent calculations and analysis.

- Define Hierarchies and KPIs: Power Pivot supports the creation of hierarchies and Key Performance Indicators (KPIs), enhancing data organization and enabling better insights into data trends and performance.

Step 3: Data Analysis and Calculations with DAX

- Perform Calculations: DAX expressions can be used to create calculated columns and measures in the data model, allowing users to perform calculations based on specific business logic and requirements.

- Time Intelligence: DAX offers a wide range of time intelligence functions that enable users to perform dynamic calculations based on time periods, such as year-to-date, quarter-to-date, and rolling averages.

Step 4: Data Visualization and Reporting

- Interactive Reports and Dashboards: Power BI's visualization capabilities allow users to create interactive and visually appealing reports and dashboards. Users can add charts, tables, maps, and other visuals to present data and insights effectively.

- Data Exploration: With slicers, cross-filtering, and drill-down capabilities, users can explore data from different angles, gain deeper insights, and make data-driven decisions.

9.3.3 Leveraging the Synergy of DAX, Power Query, and Power Pivot

The synergy between DAX, Power Query, and Power Pivot offers several advantages for data analysis in Power BI:

1. Comprehensive Data Preparation: Power Query simplifies data preparation by providing a user-friendly interface for connecting to data sources, transforming data, and loading it into Power Pivot. This ensures that the data model is clean, accurate, and ready for analysis.

2. Efficient Data Modeling: Power Pivot's in-memory data model enables fast data retrieval and calculations, even with large datasets. The ability to define relationships between tables allows users to create a structured and organized data model that accurately represents the business scenario.

3. Advanced Calculations and Insights: DAX extends the analytical capabilities of Power Pivot by enabling users to perform complex calculations and create custom measures. Time intelligence functions in DAX provide dynamic insights based on time periods, facilitating trend analysis and comparisons.

4. Interactive Data Exploration: Power BI's interactive visualizations empower users to explore data and gain insights through various interactions. The combination of slicers, cross-filtering, and drill-downs enables a deeper understanding of data and facilitates data-driven decision-making.

9.3.4 Real-World Applications

The integration of DAX, Power Query, and Power Pivot in Power BI finds applications in various real-world scenarios:

- Business Performance Analysis: Power BI can be used to analyze sales data, customer behavior, and financial performance. With DAX, users can

calculate key performance indicators and conduct trend analysis to identify growth opportunities and areas for improvement.

- Financial Reporting: Power BI's integration with Power Query and Power Pivot simplifies financial reporting tasks. Users can consolidate financial data from different departments, create interactive financial reports, and track financial performance using custom calculations.

- Data Exploration and Insights: Power BI's interactive visuals and DAX calculations facilitate data exploration and uncover hidden insights. Users can identify patterns, anomalies, and trends that may not be apparent in traditional static reports.

- Time Series Analysis: DAX's time intelligence functions enable users to perform time series analysis and compare data across different time periods. This is particularly valuable for sales forecasting, inventory management, and demand planning.

9.3.5 Conclusion

The seamless integration of DAX, Power Query, and Power Pivot in Power BI provides a powerful data analysis and visualization platform. By combining data preparation, data modeling, and advanced calculations, users can transform raw data into meaningful insights and create interactive reports and dashboards that support data-driven decision-making.

Understanding the role and capabilities of DAX, Power Query, and Power Pivot and knowing how to effectively combine these components are essential for maximizing the potential of Power BI and harnessing its capabilities for a wide range of data analysis scenarios. As we continue our journey with Power BI, we will delve deeper into advanced techniques and features that further enhance data modeling and analysis in Power BI.

CHAPTER X
Optimizing Performance with DAX

10.1 Optimizing DAX Formulas for Improved Performance

In this chapter, we will focus on optimizing the performance of DAX formulas in Power BI to enhance the overall efficiency and responsiveness of data analysis. As datasets grow in size and complexity, DAX calculations can sometimes slow down, affecting the user experience and report generation time. By understanding the factors that impact DAX performance and implementing optimization techniques, users can significantly improve the responsiveness of their Power BI reports and dashboards.

10.1.1 Understanding DAX Performance

DAX is a powerful formula language that allows users to create complex calculations and measures in Power BI. While DAX provides tremendous flexibility and analytical capabilities, poorly constructed formulas or large datasets can lead to suboptimal performance.

DAX performance is influenced by several factors, including:

1. Formula Complexity: The complexity of DAX formulas can impact performance. Highly complex calculations may require more processing time, especially when dealing with large datasets.

2. Data Model Size: The size of the data model and the number of rows in tables can affect DAX performance. As the data model grows, DAX calculations may take longer to complete.

3. Relationship Cardinality: The cardinality of relationships between tables can impact DAX performance. Many-to-many relationships or large one-to-many relationships may slow down calculations.

4. Context Transition: DAX operates in different contexts, such as row context and filter context. Understanding and managing context transitions is crucial for optimal DAX performance.

10.1.2 Techniques for Optimizing DAX Formulas

To optimize DAX formulas and improve performance, users can implement the following techniques:

1. Use SUMX Instead of SUM: In scenarios where SUM is used with filters or iterators, consider using SUMX. SUMX can be more efficient when calculating totals over filtered rows.

2. Avoid Using Implicit Measures: Implicit measures are automatically generated when users drag fields onto visuals. While convenient, they may result in redundant calculations. Creating explicit measures allows users to control the logic and optimize performance.

3. Use Variables: Variables in DAX can improve readability and performance by storing intermediate results. This avoids redundant calculations and simplifies complex formulas.

4. Reduce Row Context Operations: Row context operations, such as iterating over rows, can be computationally expensive. Minimizing row context operations can significantly improve DAX performance.

5. Simplify DAX Logic: Complex DAX formulas may involve multiple iterations and context transitions. Simplifying DAX logic by breaking down complex expressions into smaller, more manageable components can lead to better performance.

6. Optimize Relationships: Analyze the relationships between tables in the data model and consider using bi-directional filtering only when necessary. Properly defining relationships and avoiding unnecessary bi-directional filters can improve calculation efficiency.

7. Use Iterator Functions Wisely: Iterator functions, such as FILTER and ALL, can be powerful but may introduce performance overhead. Limit their use to specific scenarios and avoid applying them unnecessarily.

10.1.3 Managing Large Datasets

As datasets grow in size, managing DAX performance becomes crucial. To optimize performance with large datasets:

1. Use DirectQuery or Aggregation: For exceptionally large datasets, consider using DirectQuery mode or pre-aggregating data in the data source. This reduces the amount of data loaded into Power BI, enhancing performance.

2. Implement Data Partitioning: Partitioning data tables can improve DAX performance by limiting the amount of data processed during calculations.

3. Utilize Data Compression: Power BI's data compression techniques can reduce the memory footprint and enhance DAX calculation efficiency.

10.1.4 Performance Monitoring and Analysis

Monitoring DAX performance is essential to identify bottlenecks and opportunities for improvement. Users can employ the following techniques:

1. Performance Analyzer: Power BI's Performance Analyzer tool allows users to analyze query and rendering times for visuals and measures, identifying potential performance issues.

2. Query Diagnostics: Using the Query Diagnostics feature, users can capture and analyze query execution times, helping to pinpoint areas for optimization.

3. Query Reduction: Reducing the number of queries executed can improve performance. Combine visuals, use bookmarks, and minimize slicer selections to reduce redundant queries.

10.1.5 Testing and Iterative Optimization

Optimizing DAX performance is an iterative process. After applying optimization techniques, it is essential to test the impact of changes on performance and user experience. Users can use Power BI's performance testing capabilities to compare report load times and response times before and after optimization.

By testing and iterating on optimization strategies, users can achieve a fine-tuned data model with efficient DAX calculations, resulting in responsive and interactive Power BI reports.

10.1.6 Conclusion

Optimizing DAX formulas is crucial for enhancing the performance of Power BI reports and dashboards. Understanding the factors that impact DAX performance and implementing optimization techniques can significantly improve data analysis responsiveness and user experience.

By using variables, simplifying DAX logic, and reducing row context operations, users can streamline complex calculations and avoid unnecessary overhead. Properly managing large datasets through data partitioning, compression, and utilizing DirectQuery or aggregation can further enhance DAX performance.

Regular performance monitoring, testing, and iterative optimization are essential to maintaining an efficient data model and ensuring responsive Power BI reports. By continuously fine-tuning DAX formulas and data modeling techniques, users can leverage the full potential of Power BI for impactful data analysis and visualization.

10.2 Using Variables and Tables in DAX

In this section, we will explore the powerful capabilities of using variables and tables in Data Analysis Expressions (DAX) to optimize performance and improve the readability of DAX formulas. Variables and tables allow users to store intermediate results, simplify complex calculations, and enhance code reusability, leading to more efficient and maintainable DAX expressions in Power BI.

10.2.1 Introducing Variables in DAX

Variables in DAX serve as containers to hold temporary values or expressions that can be referenced throughout a DAX formula. They are created using the "VAR" keyword, followed by the variable name, an equal sign, and the expression to be stored. Variables are used to break down complex formulas into smaller, more manageable parts, making DAX logic easier to read and maintain.

The syntax for creating a variable in DAX is as follows:

```
```

```
VAR variable_name = expression
```


For example, let's consider a DAX formula that calculates the total sales for a specific product and period. Without using variables, the formula might look like this:


```
CALCULATE(

    SUM('Sales'[Amount]),

    FILTER('Sales', 'Sales'[Product] = "Product A" && 'Sales'[Date] >= DATE(2023, 1, 1) && 'Sales'[Date] <= DATE(2023, 12, 31))

)
```


By using variables, we can rewrite the formula to improve readability:

```
VAR SelectedProduct = "Product A"

VAR StartDate = DATE(2023, 1, 1)

VAR EndDate = DATE(2023, 12, 31)


CALCULATE(

    SUM('Sales'[Amount]),

    FILTER('Sales', 'Sales'[Product] = SelectedProduct && 'Sales'[Date] >= StartDate && 'Sales'[Date] <= EndDate)

)
```

Using variables not only simplifies the formula but also makes it easier to adjust the selected product and date range without modifying the entire expression.

10.2.2 Benefits of Using Variables

Using variables in DAX offers several benefits:

1. Improved Readability: By breaking down complex expressions into smaller pieces, variables enhance the readability of DAX formulas. This makes it easier for other users to understand the logic behind the calculations.

2. Enhanced Maintainability: Variables provide a structured approach to DAX programming, making it easier to troubleshoot and modify formulas. Changes can be made to individual variables without affecting the rest of the formula.

3. Reusability: Variables can be reused across different parts of the formula or in other measures, promoting code reusability and reducing redundant calculations.

4. Performance Optimization: Variables can lead to better DAX performance by storing intermediate results and avoiding repeated calculations.

10.2.3 Using Tables in DAX

In addition to variables, DAX allows users to create virtual tables using the "SUMMARIZE" and "ADDCOLUMNS" functions. These virtual tables can then be referenced in DAX calculations to simplify complex expressions and enhance performance.

The "SUMMARIZE" function creates a summary table that groups data based on specified columns and calculates aggregations. The syntax for the "SUMMARIZE" function is as follows:

```
SUMMARIZE(Table, [GroupBy_Column1, GroupBy_Column2, ...], [Aggregation_Column1, Aggregation_Column2, ...])
```

For example, let's say we want to create a summary table that groups sales data by product and calculates the total sales and average price for each product. The DAX formula using the "SUMMARIZE" function would be as follows:

```
SUMMARIZE(
    'Sales',
    'Sales'[Product],
    "Total Sales", SUM('Sales'[Amount]),
    "Average Price", AVERAGE('Sales'[Price])
)
```

The "ADDCOLUMNS" function allows users to add new columns to an existing table, based on expressions specified in the DAX formula. The syntax for the "ADDCOLUMNS" function is as follows:

```
ADDCOLUMNS(Table, [New_Column1, New_Column2, ...], [Expression1, Expression2, ...])
```

```
```

For example, let's say we want to add a new column to the sales table that calculates the profit margin for each transaction. The DAX formula using the "ADDCOLUMNS" function would be as follows:

```
```

ADDCOLUMNS(

   'Sales',

   "Profit Margin", DIVIDE('Sales'[Profit], 'Sales'[Amount])

)
```
```

By using tables in DAX, users can simplify complex calculations, create custom aggregations, and enhance the performance of data analysis in Power BI.

10.2.4 Combining Variables and Tables in DAX

The true power of DAX optimization lies in the combination of variables and tables. By using variables to store intermediate results and

creating virtual tables to summarize data, users can build efficient and concise DAX formulas.

For example, let's consider a scenario where we want to calculate the sales growth rate for each product over a specific period. We can use variables to store the start and end dates, and then create a virtual table using the "SUMMARIZE" function to calculate the total sales for each product in both the current and previous periods. Finally, we can use these intermediate results in the main calculation to calculate the sales growth rate.

```
```

VAR StartDate = DATE(2023, 1, 1)

VAR EndDate = DATE(2023, 12, 31)

VAR SalesCurrentPeriod = SUMMARIZE(

    FILTER('Sales', 'Sales'[Date] >= StartDate && 'Sales'[Date] <= EndDate),

    'Sales'[Product],

    "Total Sales Current Period", SUM('Sales'[Amount])

)

VAR SalesPreviousPeriod = SUMMARIZE(

    FILTER('Sales', 'Sales'[Date] >= StartDate && 'Sales'[Date] <= EndDate - 365),

    'Sales'[Product],

    "Total Sales Previous Period", SUM('Sales'[Amount])

)

CALCULATE(

    DIVIDE(

        SUMX(SalesCurrentPeriod, [Total Sales Current Period]),

        SUMX(SalesPreviousPeriod, [Total Sales Previous Period])

) - 1,

    ALL('Sales'[Product])

)

```
```

In this example, the use of variables and virtual tables allows us to perform the necessary calculations efficiently, resulting in a clean and optimized DAX formula.

10.2.5 Conclusion

Using variables and tables in DAX is a powerful technique for optimizing performance and improving the readability of DAX formulas in Power BI. By storing intermediate results, breaking down complex expressions, and creating virtual tables, users can streamline DAX calculations and enhance the efficiency of data analysis.

By leveraging the capabilities of variables and tables, users can unlock the full potential of DAX and create responsive and insightful Power BI reports and dashboards for data-driven decision-making.

10.3 Tips and Tricks for Handling Large Data Volumes

In this section, we will explore practical tips and tricks for effectively handling large data volumes in Power BI while optimizing the performance of DAX calculations. As datasets grow in size, the efficiency of DAX formulas becomes critical to ensure responsive and smooth data analysis and visualization. By implementing the following strategies, users can manage large data volumes and enhance the overall performance of their Power BI reports and dashboards.

10.3.1 Data Model Optimization

Optimizing the data model is a crucial step in handling large data volumes in Power BI. Users should focus on the following aspects to improve data model efficiency:

1. Data Partitioning: Divide large tables into smaller partitions based on specific criteria, such as date ranges or geographical regions. Data partitioning allows Power BI to load and process only the relevant data, reducing the memory footprint and improving performance.

2. Aggregation: Pre-aggregate data where appropriate to reduce the number of rows in the data model. Aggregating data at higher levels can speed up calculations and reporting.

3. Composite Models: Utilize composite models to combine in-memory and DirectQuery storage modes. This approach allows users to keep essential data in memory while offloading less frequently used data to DirectQuery mode.

4. Data Compression: Enable data compression in the data model to reduce memory usage without sacrificing performance. Power BI's built-in compression techniques can significantly optimize storage.

5. Disable Auto Date/Time: For large datasets, consider disabling the Auto Date/Time feature in Power BI, as it automatically creates date tables, which might not be necessary for all scenarios.

10.3.2 Efficient Query Design

Efficient query design is essential to ensure that DAX calculations run smoothly with large data volumes. Consider the following practices for query optimization:

1. Minimize Cross Filtering: Cross filtering between tables can create complex relationships that impact query performance. Limit cross filtering to necessary scenarios and avoid excessive bi-directional filtering.

2. Avoid Cartesian Joins: Cartesian joins result from relationships with no unique keys or when relationships are missing. Cartesian joins can lead to bloated intermediate results and slow down calculations.

3. Optimize Filter Context: Be mindful of the filter context when designing DAX calculations. Inappropriate filter context can cause excessive calculations and reduce performance.

10.3.3 Partitioned Tables and Incremental Refresh

For exceptionally large datasets, consider implementing partitioned tables and incremental refresh to enhance data loading and processing:

1. Partitioned Tables: Divide large tables into partitions based on a specific column (e.g., date) to allow for faster data loading and querying. Each partition operates independently, leading to improved performance.

2. Incremental Refresh: Use incremental refresh to load only new or modified data into the data model instead of reloading the entire dataset. Incremental refresh reduces data loading time and improves efficiency.

10.3.4 Use DirectQuery Mode

For extremely large datasets that exceed the memory capacity of Power BI, consider using DirectQuery mode. DirectQuery allows data to be queried directly from the underlying data source, bypassing in-memory storage. This approach offloads data processing to the data source, resulting in improved performance for large datasets.

10.3.5 Consider Data Summarization

When dealing with vast datasets, consider summarizing the data before importing it into Power BI. Pre-aggregating data at the source can significantly reduce the volume of data imported into the data model, leading to faster query performance.

10.3.6 Limit Visualizations and Data Points

To avoid overwhelming the data model and ensure responsive reporting, limit the number of visuals and data points on each page. Too many visuals or data points can strain system resources and affect performance, especially with large datasets.

10.3.7 Use Performance Analyzer and Query Diagnostics

Leverage Power BI's Performance Analyzer and Query Diagnostics features to analyze and identify performance bottlenecks in DAX calculations. These tools provide insights into query execution times, helping users pinpoint areas for optimization.

10.3.8 Regular Testing and Monitoring

Regularly test and monitor the performance of Power BI reports and dashboards to identify potential issues and ensure continued efficiency. Perform tests with different data volumes and user scenarios to gauge responsiveness.

10.3.9 Conclusion

Handling large data volumes in Power BI requires a combination of data model optimization, efficient query design, and thoughtful partitioning and refresh strategies. By implementing best practices, such as data partitioning, aggregation, and compression, users can optimize DAX calculations and ensure that Power BI reports remain responsive, even with massive datasets.

Using DirectQuery mode and incremental refresh for exceptionally large datasets can further improve performance, while performance monitoring tools help identify areas for optimization.

By applying these tips and tricks for handling large data volumes, users can unlock the full potential of Power BI and deliver high-performance data analysis and visualization solutions to support data-driven decision-making across the organization.

CHAPTER XI
Real-World Applications and Practical Exercises

11.1 Applying DAX Functions in Real Data Analysis Scenarios

In this chapter, we will explore real-world applications of Data Analysis Expressions (DAX) functions in Power BI. DAX provides a powerful toolkit for performing complex calculations and analysis on data, making it a valuable asset in various data-driven scenarios. We will delve into practical examples of how DAX functions can be leveraged to solve common data analysis challenges and gain valuable insights from real datasets.

11.1.1 Sales Performance Analysis

One of the most common applications of DAX is sales performance analysis. Organizations often need to assess their sales performance across different products, regions, or time periods to identify trends and growth opportunities. DAX functions like SUM, AVERAGE, and CALCULATE are fundamental for aggregating sales data and calculating metrics such as total revenue, average sales, and year-over-year growth.

For example, let's consider a sales dataset with columns for Product, Region, Date, and Sales Amount. We can use DAX functions to calculate the total sales for each product, the average sales by region, and the year-over-year growth rate. The CALCULATE and FILTER functions enable us to apply specific filters and date ranges for these calculations.

11.1.2 Financial Analysis and KPIs

DAX is well-suited for financial analysis, where key performance indicators (KPIs) and financial ratios play a crucial role in decision-making. DAX functions like DIVIDE, SUMX, and RELATED allow us to calculate financial metrics such as profit margin, return on investment (ROI), and net present value (NPV).

For instance, let's consider a financial dataset with columns for Revenue, Expenses, and Profit. We can use DAX to calculate the profit margin as the percentage of profit over revenue. The DIVIDE function comes in handy to perform this calculation.

11.1.3 Time Series Analysis

Time series analysis is essential for understanding data patterns and making predictions based on historical trends. DAX provides a range of time intelligence functions like TOTALYTD, SAMEPERIODLASTYEAR, and DATESYTD to analyze data over different time periods.

For example, let's consider a dataset with columns for Date, Sales, and Expenses. Using DAX functions, we can calculate year-to-date (YTD) sales and expenses, compare them with the same period last year, and analyze year-over-year growth.

11.1.4 Customer Segmentation and Cohort Analysis

DAX can also be employed for customer segmentation and cohort analysis, which help businesses understand customer behavior and preferences. DAX functions like COUNTROWS, FILTER, and SUMMARIZE enable us to group customers based on specific criteria and analyze their behavior over time.

For instance, let's consider a customer dataset with columns for CustomerID, Date of First Purchase, and Total Purchases. We can use DAX to segment customers into different cohorts based on their first purchase date and calculate the total purchases for each cohort.

11.1.5 Inventory Management and Demand Forecasting

For businesses dealing with inventory management, DAX can assist in calculating inventory turnover, reorder points, and demand forecasting. DAX functions like AVERAGEX, SUMMARIZE, and MAX help analyze historical inventory data and make informed decisions on stock levels.

For example, let's consider an inventory dataset with columns for Product, Date, and Stock Quantity. Using DAX, we can calculate the average inventory turnover and forecast demand based on historical sales data.

11.1.6 HR and Employee Performance Analysis

In the context of human resources, DAX can be used to analyze employee performance, track key HR metrics, and evaluate workforce productivity. DAX functions like COUNTA, RANKX, and SWITCH enable us to assess employee performance and identify top performers.

For instance, let's consider an employee dataset with columns for EmployeeID, Department, Date of Joining, and Performance Rating. Using DAX, we can calculate the number of employees in each department, rank employees based on performance, and analyze employee turnover over time.

11.1.7 Practical Exercises

To reinforce the understanding of DAX functions and their applications, we provide practical exercises for readers to complete. These exercises involve working with real datasets and solving specific data analysis challenges using DAX.

The exercises cover various scenarios, including sales analysis, financial calculations, time series analysis, customer segmentation, and inventory management. Each exercise presents a specific problem to solve, guiding readers to apply relevant DAX functions to derive meaningful insights.

Through these practical exercises, readers can gain hands-on experience with DAX and build confidence in using DAX functions effectively in their data analysis projects.

11.1.8 Conclusion

DAX functions are a powerful asset in Power BI, enabling users to perform complex calculations and gain valuable insights from real data. By applying DAX functions in real-world scenarios, such as sales performance analysis, financial calculations, time series analysis, customer segmentation, and inventory management, users can unleash the full potential of Power BI for data-driven decision-making.

The practical exercises provided in this chapter offer readers an opportunity to sharpen their DAX skills and apply DAX functions to solve common data analysis challenges. By mastering DAX, users can become proficient in handling diverse data analysis scenarios and transforming raw data into actionable insights.

11.2 Creating Smart Reports and Charts with DAX

In this section, we will delve into the art of creating smart and insightful reports and charts using Data Analysis Expressions (DAX) in Power BI. DAX is a powerful formula language that enables users to perform complex calculations, define custom metrics, and design dynamic visualizations. By harnessing the capabilities of DAX, users can elevate their data analysis and visualization to new heights, providing stakeholders with actionable insights and facilitating data-driven decision-making.

11.2.1 Understanding Measures and Calculated Columns

Measures and calculated columns are essential components of building intelligent reports and charts in Power BI. Measures are dynamic calculations that respond to user interactions and selections, such as filtering and slicing data. On the other hand, calculated columns introduce new data based on existing columns and remain static throughout the report.

DAX functions play a central role in creating measures and calculated columns. Functions like SUM, AVERAGE, COUNT, and DIVIDE are fundamental for aggregating data and performing basic calculations. More advanced functions like IF, SWITCH, RELATED, and FILTER enable users to perform conditional calculations, establish relationships between tables, and apply customized filtering logic.

For example, in a sales dataset with columns for Product, Region, Date, and Sales Amount, we can create measures using DAX functions to calculate total sales, average sales, and year-over-year growth. These measures will automatically adjust based on user interactions, such as selecting specific products or date ranges.

11.2.2 Dynamic Visualization with DAX

DAX empowers users to design dynamic visualizations that adapt in real-time to user interactions and selections. By utilizing measures and DAX functions, reports and charts can respond intelligently, providing instant insights as users explore the data.

For instance, a line chart can be created to display sales trends over time. By using a dynamic measure that calculates total sales based on the selected date range, the chart will automatically adjust to display the relevant data as the user changes the date filter. This dynamic behavior allows stakeholders to gain deeper insights into sales patterns across different time periods effortlessly.

Similarly, a bar chart can be designed to showcase the top-performing products based on the selected region. By employing DAX functions to rank products based on sales, the bar chart will dynamically update to reflect the current top products for the chosen region. This interactive visualization facilitates quick and accurate analysis of regional product performance.

11.2.3 Hierarchies and Drill-Downs

Hierarchies and drill-down capabilities are powerful features enabled by DAX, providing users with the ability to explore data at various levels of granularity. Hierarchies allow users to view data at different aggregation levels, such as year, quarter, month, and day.

For example, a date hierarchy can be established using DAX functions to group data by year, quarter, month, and day. Users can then drill down from yearly data to quarterly, monthly, and daily data, gaining a deeper understanding of sales trends over time. This drill-down capability empowers stakeholders to uncover granular insights and detect seasonal trends or anomalies.

11.2.4 Time Intelligence and Comparative Analysis

Time intelligence is a critical aspect of data analysis, and DAX provides a set of powerful time-related functions to perform comparative analysis over different periods. Functions like SAMEPERIODLASTYEAR, TOTALYTD, and DATESYTD enable calculations that compare data between the current period and previous periods.

For instance, a card visualization can be created to display the year-over-year growth rate for total sales. By using DAX functions to calculate sales for the current year and the same period last year, the card visualization will dynamically show the percentage change. This time intelligence feature facilitates insightful comparisons and highlights performance trends across time.

11.2.5 Smart Filters and Slicers

DAX enables the creation of smart filters and slicers that enhance user interactivity in reports. By utilizing DAX functions in combination with slicers, users can make data selections that dynamically update the visualizations on the report canvas.

For example, a slicer can be designed to allow users to filter data by product category. By using DAX functions to apply the selected category as a filter to the visualizations, the report will adjust to display data specific to the chosen product category. This interactive filtering capability allows stakeholders to focus on specific aspects of the data for deeper analysis.

11.2.6 Advanced Analytics with DAX

Beyond basic calculations, DAX empowers users to perform sophisticated analytics using advanced functions. Functions like RANKX, PERCENTILEX.INC, and VAR enable users to derive deeper insights from the data.

For instance, a matrix visualization can be created to display the top-performing sales representatives based on total sales. By using the RANKX function, the matrix will dynamically rank sales representatives and display the top performers, aiding in identifying top sales performers efficiently.

11.2.7 Dynamic Forecasting

Forecasting is a critical aspect of data analysis, and DAX offers functions like FORECAST.ETS and FORECAST.LINEAR to create dynamic forecasting models. By leveraging these functions, users can predict future trends and make informed decisions based on the data.

For example, a line chart can be designed to show historical sales data along with a dynamic forecast of future sales. By using the FORECAST.ETS function, the line chart will dynamically display the predicted sales trend based on historical data. This dynamic forecasting feature aids in making accurate predictions and supporting data-driven decision-making.

11.2.8 Data Storytelling with DAX

DAX facilitates data storytelling by providing dynamic calculations and visualizations that convey insights effectively. By creating compelling visualizations with DAX measures and functions, users can present data-driven narratives that engage stakeholders and support decision-making.

For example, a report can be designed to tell the story of sales performance by region. By using DAX to calculate regional sales metrics and creating interactive visualizations, users can craft a data story that highlights the strengths and opportunities

in different regions. This data storytelling capability empowers stakeholders to grasp insights quickly and make informed choices for their organizations.

11.2.9 Conclusion

Creating smart reports and charts with DAX in Power BI opens up a realm of possibilities for data analysis and visualization. DAX functions allow dynamic calculations, interactive visualizations, and advanced analytics, enabling users to derive meaningful insights from their data.

By leveraging measures, calculated columns, hierarchies, and time intelligence, users can design reports that respond intelligently to user interactions and provide real-time insights. Smart filters, slicers, and forecasting capabilities enhance user interactivity and data storytelling.

With DAX as a powerful ally, users can create compelling and insightful reports and charts that drive data-driven decision-making and empower stakeholders to make informed choices for their organizations. By mastering DAX and harnessing its potential, users can transform raw data into actionable insights, revolutionizing the way data is analyzed and understood.

11.3 Step-by-Step Guidance for Practicing DAX Usage

In this section, we provide comprehensive step-by-step guidance for practicing the usage of Data Analysis Expressions (DAX) in Power BI. DAX is a powerful formula language that allows users to perform complex calculations, create custom metrics, and design dynamic reports and charts. By following the practical exercises and examples presented here, users can gain hands-on experience with DAX and sharpen their skills in real-world data analysis scenarios.

11.3.1 Setting Up the Environment

Before diving into DAX, it's essential to ensure that the Power BI environment is set up correctly. Users should have the latest version of Power BI Desktop installed on their computer. Additionally, access to relevant datasets and sample data is crucial for practicing DAX effectively.

In this section, we guide users through the process of setting up the Power BI environment and importing sample datasets. We provide step-by-step instructions on how to connect to data sources, import data, and prepare the datasets for analysis.

11.3.2 Understanding the DAX Syntax

A strong foundation in DAX syntax is essential for effective data analysis. In this part, we introduce users to the basic syntax of DAX functions and expressions. We cover fundamental elements such as functions, operators, and variables, along with rules for writing DAX formulas.

Through practical examples, users will learn how to create simple DAX calculations and apply basic functions like SUM, AVERAGE, and COUNT. We also introduce the concept of calculated columns and how they differ from measures.

11.3.3 Creating Measures with DAX

Measures are dynamic calculations that respond to user interactions and selections. In this section, we focus on creating measures using DAX functions to perform advanced calculations. Users will learn how to aggregate data using functions like SUMX, AVERAGEX, and MINX, and how to use filters with functions like FILTER and ALL.

Through step-by-step instructions, users will create measures to calculate total sales, average revenue, and year-over-year growth. We demonstrate how measures adjust dynamically as users interact with the report, providing real-time insights.

11.3.4 Time Intelligence with DAX

Time intelligence is a crucial aspect of data analysis, and DAX offers a range of functions specifically designed for time-related calculations. In this part, we introduce users to time intelligence functions like TOTALYTD, SAMEPERIODLASTYEAR, and DATESYTD.

Through practical exercises, users will learn how to create dynamic time-based calculations such as year-to-date sales, month-over-month growth, and rolling averages. They will also explore how to build date hierarchies and utilize time intelligence functions for comparative analysis over different time periods.

11.3.5 Advanced DAX Functions

Building on the foundational knowledge of DAX, we delve into more advanced functions that allow users to perform sophisticated data analysis. In this section, we introduce functions like RANKX, PERCENTILEX.INC, and SWITCH.

Through hands-on exercises, users will learn how to rank data based on specific criteria, calculate percentiles, and handle conditional logic with the SWITCH function. These advanced DAX functions expand the analytical capabilities and enable users to derive deeper insights from the data.

11.3.6 Combining DAX with Power Query and Power Pivot

Power Query and Power Pivot are integral components of Power BI that complement DAX functionality. In this part, we guide users through the process of combining DAX with Power Query for data extraction and transformation, and Power Pivot for building data models and table relationships.

Users will learn how to use Power Query to clean and shape data before importing it into Power BI. They will also understand how to create relationships between tables using Power Pivot, allowing them to leverage DAX functions across multiple data sources.

11.3.7 Dynamic Visualization and Data Storytelling

Dynamic visualizations are essential for engaging data storytelling. In this section, users will learn how to design interactive and responsive reports and charts using DAX measures and functions.

Through practical examples, users will create dynamic line charts, bar charts, and matrices that respond to user selections and filters. They will also explore smart filters and slicers that enhance interactivity, allowing stakeholders to focus on specific data points for deeper analysis.

11.3.8 Real-World Applications and Practical Exercises

To reinforce the learning process, we present real-world applications and practical exercises that challenge users to apply their knowledge of DAX in various data analysis scenarios.

Through these exercises, users will tackle data analysis challenges such as sales performance analysis, financial calculations, customer segmentation, and time series analysis. Each exercise guides users through the steps of using DAX functions to derive insights and visualize data effectively.

11.3.9 Conclusion

The step-by-step guidance provided in this section equips users with the knowledge and skills to practice DAX usage effectively in Power BI. By understanding the DAX syntax, creating measures, utilizing time intelligence, and leveraging advanced functions, users can perform complex data analysis and visualization.

Combining DAX with Power Query and Power Pivot expands the analytical capabilities, and dynamic visualization and data storytelling facilitate effective communication of insights. Through real-world applications and practical exercises, users gain hands-on experience in applying DAX to solve diverse data analysis challenges.

By mastering DAX, users can elevate their data analysis and visualization capabilities, becoming proficient in handling real-world data scenarios and transforming raw data into actionable insights. DAX empowers users to unleash the full potential of Power BI, making it an indispensable tool for data-driven decision-making and supporting business success.

As we reach the conclusion of "POWER BI DAX: A Guide to Using Basic Functions in Data Analysis," we want to express our heartfelt appreciation to each and every one of you for choosing to embark on this learning journey with us. We are truly grateful for the opportunity to be a part of your data analysis and visualization exploration.

In this book, our main objective has been to equip you with a comprehensive understanding of Data Analysis Expressions (DAX) and its role in empowering you to create intelligent reports and dynamic charts in Power BI. We sincerely hope that the knowledge and techniques shared within these pages have provided you with valuable insights and practical skills that you can apply to your own data projects.

We understand that diving into a new subject can be challenging, but we are genuinely thankful for your dedication and commitment to learning. Our aim has been to make the journey smoother for you by providing step-by-step guidance, real-world examples, and practical exercises to reinforce your understanding of DAX and its functionalities.

We would like to extend our gratitude to the entire team involved in bringing this book to life. Their passion for data analysis and visualization, combined with their expertise, has been instrumental in creating a resource we hope you find valuable.

We also want to acknowledge the Power BI community for its continuous support and inspiration. Your enthusiasm and eagerness to delve into the world of data analysis motivate us to continue contributing to your learning experience.

As you move forward with the knowledge gained from this book, we encourage you to explore and experiment with DAX further. Embrace the power of data storytelling and let your reports and charts communicate impactful insights to your audience.

Finally, we want to express our best wishes to you in all your future data endeavors. May you continue to harness the potential of DAX and Power BI to uncover hidden patterns in your data and make data-driven decisions with confidence.

Thank you once again for choosing "POWER BI DAX: A Guide to Using Basic Functions in Data Analysis" We hope that the skills and understanding you have acquired from this book will serve you well in your data analysis pursuits.

www.ingramcontent.com/pod-product-compliance
Lightning Source LLC
Chambersburg PA
CBHW080555060326
40689CB00021B/4862